I0162322

The Gospel Propeller

Christian Musician/Song Ministry

The Gospel Propeller

Copyright © 2009
Revised 2015
Author Tiffany Buckner
Email: info@anointedfire.com
Publisher's Website: www.anointedfirehouse.com

All scriptures noted in this book were taken from the NIV bible unless otherwise noted.

ISBN-13: 978-0692413395
ISBN-10: 0692413391

Disclaimer: This book is designed to provide information and motivation to our readers. It is sold with the understanding that the publisher is not engaged to render any type of psychological, legal, or any other kind of professional advice. No warranties or guarantees are expressed or implied by the author, since every man has his own measure of faith. The individual author(s) shall not be liable for any physical, psychological, emotional, financial, or commercial damages, including; but not limited to, special, incidental, consequential or other damages. Our views and rights are the same: You are responsible for your own choices, actions, and results.

Some names and identifying details have been changed to protect the privacy of individuals.

Dedication

As always, I dedicate this book to my glorious and magnificent Father in Heaven, YAHWEH. Thank You for entrusting me to birth this book in 2009, and thank You for blessing me with the ability to rebirth this book in 2015. You are my Everything, and I will never be ashamed of You. I want You to be glorified in all that I do, so I write this for the whole world and the church to see: I love you with everything in me, every fiber of my being, and every breath in my body. You are the love of my life and I adore You, my sweet and precious Father. Abba FATHER, I reverence and adore You, and I ask that You touch the hearts of everyone who reads this book, giving them Your wisdom, and blessing them to understand the assignments You've given them. Glorify Your name, beautiful, perfect, and Almighty GOD.

Introduction

Note: This book is a combination of my experiences, opinions, and some of the wisdom I've learned along the way. In some of the chapters, you'll be encouraged, whereas, in other chapters, you'll be taught. Just take in the information you need in whatever hour you're in.

Somewhere in this world another Christian Artist is sitting in his car right now holding up his cell phone. He is preparing to take another picture of himself to place on his unprofessionally designed website. He's excited about what's to come; after all, he's received many prophecies about his gospel music career. He's covered himself in expensive clothing, went and had his hair professionally cut, and he's holding up a five hundred dollar cell phone, nevertheless, he won't put a dime into his ministry. As a matter of fact, he built his website himself because he didn't want to pay a professional web designer to design it for him. Even though he's no writer, he's written his own biography, and his bio flows from first person to third person, boasting on his works, but not his anointing. He's ready for the manifestation of the prophecies he's received, but he's not willing to invest in his ministry. Nevertheless, because he takes the seed that God has given him, and he covers himself in it, his ego continues to grow, but not his ministry. Five to ten years later, he's still in the same place he was in when he'd started his ministry. The only difference is he has an album or two under his name. His album cover displays a picture he'd taken with his cell phone camera (once again), and the artwork on the cover is blotchy and blurred. He's frustrated because he hasn't earned back the *little* money he's put into producing his album, so now, he's badmouthing "church folks". "If I was a worldly Artist, I'd be sold out by now," he rants. But what he doesn't understand is in ministry, just like business, you'll only get out what you put in. Church folks aren't the problem; it's his lack mentality that's robbing him of the many opportunities that he could have enjoyed.

In the Gospel Propeller, I'm going to be straight-forward with you, and teach you about the mindsets of today's modern day church, as well as show you how you can professionally develop and promote your ministry on a budget. This book is packed with information and helpful links that will surely guide you as you build your ministry.

Table of Contents

Table of Content

My Testimony

There was a time when I was going between the church and the secular world. I tried to find ways to justify my behavior, and just like many people in the church today, I found reasonable-sounding justifications that allowed me to continue to work with the world...guilt free. It goes without saying, however, that God dealt with me, and I couldn't hide from His voice. Even though I was still somewhat young in the faith, I knew that secular music promoted a doctrine that opposed the Word of God. My favorite justification at that time was: I don't publish or promote songs with profanity or condescending lyrics, nevertheless, I was promoting music that instructed its listeners to operate in pride, to fornicate, to retaliate, and to do some pretty ungodly things.

I did not want to give up my company. After all, I'd built a website promoting secular Artists and models, and my website, although unprofessionally designed, had started garnering some popularity. I had many secular Artists reaching out to me, and many of them were looking for brand managers, A & R agents, and someone to manage their careers. I was all-too-happy to accept the new titles and bring the Artists under my broken wings because I was trying to find myself somewhere, somehow. I was trying to find success, and the secular world seemed to be the best place to find that success. I was going through a divorce, living back at my mother's house, and desperate to make a better life for myself. As you can see, my mind was set on me, and I didn't care about what effect my website would have on others. I hadn't separated myself from the world at that time because I was still marveling at the things of the world. I was still listening to secular music, and I'd evolved from being a babe in Christ to being a religious saint who practiced the traditions of the church, all the while, living the secular life I'd grown to love. To make matters worse, one of the justifications I'd often give to myself was that I was telling the Artists about Jesus, when in truth, I'd mention Him from time to time. I spent many days and nights talking with secular Artists, trying to help them with their budding careers, but God knew how to get my attention and to get me to renounce the world I was trying so hard to be a part of.

One of the Artists I often spoke with was a rapper whose career seemed to be taking off pretty quickly. I didn't manage him, but I'd designed his website, and I was promoting his music on my own site. We'd often talk about the Lord, and I found myself turning to him with the many questions I had about God, the church, and any problems I had in my personal life. He was very well versed in the bible, and his hunger for the things of God was evident. I was also hungry for the Word, so he and I became good friends, even though we spoke on the phone once every two to three weeks.

One day Robert (the Artist) called me and told me to delete his website. I was baffled. Why

3

would he want me to delete such a beautiful website? He went on to explain to me that he was completely giving his life to the Lord, and the Lord had instructed him to turn away from secular music and all things secular. I marveled at his faith because, of all the Artists I'd met, he was the most promising. He had labels looking at him, and his music was as unique as it was catchy. I didn't question Robert because he'd said the Lord told him to get rid of the site, and I knew I'd been hearing that same command given to me by God. I started telling Robert what I'd been hearing in my heart, and he told me I was definitely hearing from God. He encouraged me to follow the voice of God. I was finally ready to get rid of the site I had, and the company altogether. While Robert was still on the phone with me, I went to my computer and began to delete my website. I knew that if I didn't delete that site immediately, the enemy would begin to reason with my mind, and I'd find some new justification to keep the site. I felt a whirlwind of emotions as I deleted that website, but there was no turning back. I had

4

to get rid of it because God had not gifted me to build for the world; He'd gifted me to build for the church.

After I'd gotten rid of the site, I braced myself for the backlash I knew I'd receive. I knew I had to tell every Artist who I had been working with that I could no longer work with them, and that wasn't going to be easy because I'd developed a friendship with a few of them. I'd been their personal mentor, oftentimes, ministering to them as they'd faced the struggles of life. I was the one in their ears, telling them to make sure they'd put a gospel track on their albums. I was as double-minded as I was lost, but knowing that I could talk about the Lord to many of them made my work a lot easier.

I remember telling one of the Artists that I'd deleted my website and I would no longer be working with secular music. He was not happy with my decision at all. As a matter of fact, he was livid. I'd been working with him, trying to help him build his brand, and trying to learn how to manage his career. After all, he'd asked me to manage him, and I'd accepted that challenge, but thankfully, we had never gotten around to developing and signing any contractual agreements. We'd never finalized our plans; it was all talk. Every time I'd had a contractual agreement sent to me by an Artist, or anyone, for that matter, I'd never gotten around to signing those contracts. I now know that God was protecting me because He knew that I'd answer the call on my life.

After I'd told the Artists I'd been working with that I'd deleted my site, many of them were upset with me, but asked if they could retain me as their branding agents. Still trying to hold on to the world, I agreed, but God kept dealing with me until I finally renounced the secular world altogether. I deleted every site I could find that tied me to that world, and I accepted the adverse reactions I'd received from the people who thought I was making a foolish mistake. As the months went by, I received many tests, but I'd recognized them for what they were. One such test came during a time when I needed some extra cash to fix a car I had. I'd gotten a call from an Artist I'd previously worked with, and he was offering to pay me more than what I needed to fix my car. He wanted me to build his brand, and even though the offer was tempting, I was determined to pass the test, so I'd turned him down.

For a long time, I didn't know how God would use my gifts, but I knew He'd wake them back up again at some point. I started building Christian sites for myself, offering prayer and encouragement to anyone who needed it, but my heart wasn't in those sites. It's not that I didn't want to help anyone, but the problem was I needed help myself at that time. I needed a mind change, and God knew that it wasn't my time to encourage others when I needed encouragement myself. So, I had to live through a season of what felt like nothingness, a season where I'd spent my time studying the Word of God, and going to my day-to-day job. I didn't realize that season was beneficial to the woman God had created me to

7

be. I didn't realize that I had to be torn down before I could be built up again, because what I had allowed in my heart was nothing short of idolatry. I was too into myself, and God had to destroy that idol so that His name would be glorified.

After the seasons had changed and God had given me permission to tap back into my gifts, I'd started building websites for ministries, and that's when I began to notice a big difference in the world and the church. Needless to say, I didn't like what I was seeing. The church needed a mental makeover, and it was then that I began to recognize one of the areas that God would use me in with the church.

In 2009, the Lord finally impressed it upon my heart to write *The Gospel Propeller*. I was living in Eberbach, Germany, and I wrote the initial book, *The Gospel Propeller*, overnight. Of course, I didn't have any training writing books, and my photoshop skills were still in their infant stages, so my initial book, while informative, was a mess....to say the least. The book's cover was an embarrassment to my faith, and the poorly thrown together text was full of wit and some fairly decent advice. Needless to say, six years later, I have *finally* rewritten the book so that I can draw from my years of experience as an entrepreneur, and my ever-so-evolving faith. So, be sure to have a teachable spirit and a pure heart when reading this book because I'm going to teach you what the Lord has taught me over the years. If there's something you don't agree with, don't pass it by without praying about it. You'd be amazed at the revelations God will give you if you would only seek the answers to the questions, rather than answering the questions with your own understanding.

Encouragement

Before we proceed into the meat of the book, I want to encourage you by sharing with you some of my experiences with the traditional church. Notice that I'm referring to the church I'm speaking of as the traditional church, and not just the church. There's a reason for this. The traditional church is many of the buildings of today, and the people who see those buildings as holy establishments, rather than coming to understand that they *are* the church. The traditional church is the "church folks" that the world has come to mock on the big screen. The traditional church is the typical, hypocritical, big-hat wearing saints who curse folks out on Saturday night, and then, dance around the church building on Sunday morning. The traditional church is not the same as the people of God who walk in absolute holiness, people who practice what they preach and mean what they say.

One thing I noticed about the traditional church was the mindset. You see, when I'd worked with secular Artists, many of them didn't mind investing in what they believed in. Many of them would spend their last to build their brands and promote their music, but with the church, I noticed that even though many people had the money to invest in their song ministries, their mindsets wouldn't allow them to sow the seeds. The enemy encourages the world to build, promote, and invest in the things of darkness, but the enemy discourages the church from doing the same. He tells them that other Christians are supposed to give them what they want, and they shouldn't have to pay other believers for services. He instills fear in the hearts of believers, telling them that they could invest more once they've earned more. With the traditional church, I'd come across so many manipulative souls who couldn't get past their own selfish desires to be recognized and celebrated, and for this reason, many in the church didn't have access to the blessings of God. So, like many of the secular Artists I'd worked with, many Christian Artists

turned to the devices of the flesh:
manipulation, provocative clothing, and music
that appealed to the flesh. As a matter of fact,
many Christian Artists left the church to build
their careers in the secular realm because the
secular realm, to their understanding, looked
more promising. That's because they'd become
like Saul. Instead of obeying God and doing
what He'd commanded them to do, many
Christian Artists took the rebellious path, and
as a result, they could not hear from God. God
wanted them to repent, turn away from their
wicked ways, and be led by His Word back to
their called places, but they refused. Since they
could not hear from God, some Artists began
to turn to the world, while others turned to
ministers and ministries who scratched their
itchy ears. These Artists began giving true,
God-fearing Christian Artists a bad name, a
name in which they had not earned
themselves.

When I launched Anointed Fire Magazine, it
was my heart's desire to promote Christian
music and Christian Artists, but I was not

prepared for some of the backlash I received. Of course, this backlash didn't come from the people of God who wanted to promote the things of God. This backlash came from the traditional church, the church who followed the traditions of man, all the while, ignoring the Word of God. So many people said that Christian Artists should not be promoting their music, but instead, should stick with ministering through song in the church (building) and in their local communities. The idea of a Christian Artist having an album that was about to be released offended many religious-minded folks, and I was taken aback by what I'd seen.

One woman in particular was a leader who I'd met on Facebook. She referred to herself as a Prophetess, and even though I didn't know her personally, I'd noticed that her Facebook posts seemed to be very angry. Instead of rebuking certain behaviors found in the church, and the folks who practiced those behaviors, I'd noticed that she'd pretty much written off the entire church altogether. She'd always rant on her posts about the church leadership, and I'd never seen her trying to encourage anyone or win any souls for the Lord. Instead, she was leading people away from the church and not towards the Lord. I noticed that many of the people who liked her posts seemed to be following her, and "her ministry"; after all, her words always led them back to herself.

One day, I'd posted up an advertisement, telling people about the Artist I was featuring in Anointed Fire Magazine that month, and immediately after my post went up, she published a post. In her post, she was pretty much rebuking Christian Artists who promoted their music in any way. She was basically telling the Artists that it was okay to make CDs, but they should not sell those CDs. Instead, they were to give them away. I remember clicking on her photo and noticing how dark her eyes were to me. There was something not right about that woman, and as I was looking at her photo, the Lord led me to look at the music section of her Facebook profile. In the music section, I noticed that she mainly listened to secular Artists. I was outraged. She didn't mind the church or the world enriching secular Artists, Artists who were defiling the church and perverting the minds of their listeners, but she had a problem with anyone enriching Christian Artists. She didn't want the gospel of Jesus Christ to be shared around the world. She was there to silence the men and women of God, and from that moment on, I started investigating some of the people who were against Christian Artists promoting their music. In one hundred percent of those cases, I'd found that the people were secular Christian leaders who loved the music of the world, but did not want to pay a Christian Artist to minister to or entertain them. They saw the church as a place where they could go to gather the things they needed, but they saw the world as a place they could go to sow what they'd gotten from God, and to reap the things they wanted. For this reason, I want to encourage you with your ministry. I wanted to share that testimony with you because I know that so many of you are going to come face-to-face with many demonic spirits as you build the ministry God has given you, and many of those faces who confront you will belong to people wearing religious titles. Make no mistake about it...the enemy has gotten into the traditional church, and that's why you can't follow the traditions of man. You have to be the church God has created you to be, and your heart must be pure before God so that you won't try to draw souls to yourself. With ministry, the goal is to draw souls to the Lord. Of course, there are many Christian Artists who are nothing more than secular Artists singing Christian songs, and they're doing this to build their careers. But as men and women of God, you should never look to your ministry as your career. Instead, your ministry is your assignment from God in the realm of the earth. When you start to refer to your song ministry as your career, you'll begin to think and act as the world, and that's when you'll start using Christian music to promote yourself. It's easy to cross the blurred lines behind secularism and the church, but a pure heart will always keep you on God's side. You can't be distracted by the religious souls you'll meet along the way. Instead, you have to repeatedly remind yourself that there is a difference between the traditional church and the true church, but you can't differentiate the two using your naked eyes. Sometimes, you have to pray and ask God to let you see people through His eyes, but you've got to be prepared for what He shows you. A lot of people who've prayed that prayer have had their hearts broken by what they'd seen. If God told you to build that song ministry and promote it, then you'd better obey Him, and not man. You see, God's not looking to promote you; He's looking to promote Himself through you, and that's why it's important to draw souls to Him and not yourself. The more souls He sees that He can entrust you to lead, the more souls He'll send to you.

In this book, I'm going to teach you how to promote the God in you, so this book will be offensive to secular Christians or Artists looking to grow their own names and careers. My hope is that if you've been thrown off track with your desire to promote the Lord through

your music, this book will help you to find
your way back to God's will for your ministry.

Your Physical Appearance

Your image plays a very important role in your ministry. How you look, speak, and act are all a part of your image. As a matter of fact, many Artists look for ways to create their own identities so that their styles can become their own personal trademarks. This is okay, but you've got to remember (as you'll see me elaborate throughout this book) that it's not about you garnering fame; it's about the Lord. As you lift Him up, He will lift you up, but if you promote yourself, the world will accept you, but they won't accept the Lord. That's where the term "celebrity" comes in because the word "celebrity" means "celebrated one". We have to remember that we are to lift up the name of the Lord, and ensure that everyone who follows our ministries are celebrating God and not ourselves. At the same time, we have to remember that our images will sometimes draw people to God or repel people from Him. Let's be careful when developing an identity or a brand for ourselves, remembering always to lift up the name of the Lord and not our own names.

Your Look

Ask yourself this: What does my image say to the world? We are supposed to bring the lost back to GOD, but what if your image indicates that you are lost? How many people do you think you'll be able to convince to follow the God you claim to serve? Case and point: The world came out with baggy clothes, sagging pants (*which were originally a way for homosexuals in prison to let others know they were gay*), big chains, and metal teeth or grills. Why has this been brought into the church? Aren't we supposed to be influencing the world and not be influenced by them? What if JESUS were to come back today dressed like that? How many of us would believe He was JESUS and follow Him? What does this image say to the world? They already believe that the church is full of hypocrites, and that's because it is, but we have to be the ones who change their minds about us.

Your Physical Appearance

I remember uploading biographies for a lot
of secular Artists to my old website, and most
of them had something in common, something
that they saw as stepping stones, and that was:
most of them had started off in the church. Many
secular Artists see the church as a bridge that
will help them further their careers, and for a
long time, it has been. That's because many
leaders allow secular songs, beats, dancing,
and the like into their churches. And when
other aspiring secular Artists see our soldiers
bouncing around on the church's stage,
wearing camouflage, big chains, and unlaced
sneakers, it says to them that we are aspiring to
be like them, so why would they aspire to be
like us? Why would they want to change and
give their lives to the LORD when our
mannerisms, clothes, and language reflect the
world they're accustomed to? Have you ever
witnessed this atrocity while sitting next to a
worldly Artist in church or at a religious
concert? The Artist's response is almost always
the same: a bounce of the head to show his
approval for the "Christian" Artist's style of
music, and sometimes, you'll hear secular

Artists say things like, "Church boy got skills." That's because they recognize that the church is conforming to their mindsets and ways, so they don't want to be transformed into the people who have conformed to their ways. **Romans 12:2:** And be not conformed to this world: but be ye transformed by the renewing of your mind, that ye may prove what is that good, and acceptable, and perfect, will of God.

We have got to take back the house of God and stop lending it to foolishness. Right now, the Christian faith is being made a mockery of, and many in the traditional church have contributed to this mockery. Our pastors are bouncing around on the church's stages, trying to impress the world and the youth who are following the world, not understanding that we are not supposed to be led into the world, but instead, we are to lead the world back to Christ. Nevertheless, the world *appears* to have more to offer than the church, so many people in the church are trying to bring the world into the church for the sake of making a name for themselves.

Your Physical Appearance

Your look will minister to others before you
have a chance to open your mouth, and that's
why you'll see so many Christian Artists out
today who try to defend their secular looks.
The truth is, holiness is not something you can
hide, for it is a light that draws man to Christ,
but when an Artist has to defend his or her
look, it's more than likely because neither the
world nor the church can see the light of God's
glory in them. *They can't see that light because
it's not there.* For this reason, they have to
convince the church and the world that they
are truly men and women after God's own
heart, nevertheless, their choice of ensemble
reflects their hearts' conditions. Any person
who is a friend of the world is an enemy of
God *(see James 4:4).* At the same time, we can't
serve two Gods. We are either of the world,
and our clothes and speech will reflect that, or
we are of the Lord, and our clothes and speech
will reflect that. Secularism *(worldliness)* is
something that's hard to hide because we often
speak, reason, and behave in accordance with
whatever we've been submerging our hearts in.
So, when you see, for example, a hip-hop

Christian who wears pride and sagging jeans as his trademark, you are seeing a secular man who sings Christian songs. We've got to come to understand that we are either for God or for the world, and if we are for the world, we are against God. We can't bring secularism into the church, but we can bring the Word to the secular world so we can bring some of the souls out of it. There is no bridge to be built between the world and the church, but many Artists and leaders today are building bridges for themselves to cross over from the church to the world, and from the world to the church. The ones who cross over from the world do so with the intentions of leading the church into the world.

Your Clothing

The best ensemble to display is one that shows who you are with Christ, or, in other words, clothing that represents your anointing. You don't necessarily have to look like everyone else if you are striving to create your own unique look, but you shouldn't look for ways to stand out physically; instead, simply be your own unique self and your gifting will make room for you. Your anointing will set you apart from the rest.

One great thing that you can do is link up with others who are trying to build their brands; for example, find men and women of God who are trying to create and build their clothing lines. If you can find a local fashion designer, you've done well. Offer to model their clothes in your photo shoots, and at any major events that you'll be ministering in. Please know that most designers will want their clothes back once you've worn them, so make sure you return them promptly to ensure that the designer will continue to work with you. Discuss your style with the designer, making sure to look through what they've already created, and if you can, mix and match what's already designed, rather than asking them to create something for you. Now, if you're paying the designer, you can, of course, tell them how you want the clothes designed, but if you're not paying them, you'll only offend them if you try to get them to create your own new look because your style will probably not be their own style. Every fashion designer has an area or multiple areas of design that they are comfortable with, and when you attempt to take them outside their comfort zones, you may end up offending them.

When wearing pieces designed by a local or national designer, always display the designer's name and website wherever you wear their clothes. After all, that's the exchange they're making with you. They want to bring attention to their clothing line, and if any designer feels that you are not promoting their line, they will stop allowing you to wear their clothes freely.

When choosing a fashion designer, be sure to work with Christian designers who design respectable attire. Never work with secular designers or Christian designers who make profane or seductive clothing, as people will find themselves distracted by your designer's portfolio. Wear clothing that the traditional church and the true church would have no problem promoting within the four walls of the sanctuary.

A great place to find fashion designers who are looking to build their portfolios is at some of the local colleges and universities. You can call some of the schools that offer fashion programs, and see if any of the professors would be willing to allow one or more of their students to work with you. You can also check online, especially on some of the social media websites like Facebook, Twitter, or Instagram. It is better to work with a local designer so they can measure you and you can pick up the clothes, rather than working with someone states away from you, and having to have them ship the clothes to you.

Always avoid goth-like looks, as they promote witchcraft, and not the Lord. Additionally, avoid wearing clothing that promotes what the preacher preaches against; for example: beer, cigarettes, lewdness, and so on.

Shoes

One of the biggest mistakes many song Artists make is choosing the shoes that look good to them, without considering how those shoes will feel once they're on stage. Please know that the shoes you wear will make or break your attitude. If your feet hurt, you're not going to minister to the people of God in love. Instead, you'll be moody, rushed, and abrasive. Always choose comfort over appearance, but if you can find some comfortable, good-looking shoes, get them.

Accessories
Always make sure your accessories are stylish and uncommon. Look for people who create jewelry, and make sure that you purchase your own uniquely designed pieces from them. You can ask to model their jewelry in exchange for promoting them, but most jewelry makers won't agree to such a deal because jewelry is small and most people won't notice it. All the same, jewelry is easy to lose, so most jewelry-makers won't take the risk of creating jewelry that they'll likely never see again. If you can find someone who's willing to barter with you,

be sure to advertise their names, jewelry, and websites when you are wearing their pieces.

Avoid bulky or flashy jewelry that may serve as distractions. Try to remain stylish and wear jewelry that complements the clothes you are wearing. Also avoid wearing sunglasses in the sanctuary or during the times when you're ministering through song. Sunglasses often say to the viewers that you're cocky, pride-filled, and motivated by selfish ambition. If you're dressing or behaving inappropriately, you will send many folks back into the world, and that's the opposite of being a minister of God. You want to draw souls to Christ, not send them away from Him.

Cosmetics

Ladies, when wearing makeup, try to always wear it modestly. Too much makeup distracts people from the message and causes them to focus on you. If you're not trying to draw souls to yourself, you've got to avoid wearing flashy clothing, flashy accessories, or excessive makeup. Always remember that ninety-nine to one hundred percent of your audience has vision, and oftentimes, when one of a person's senses is heightened, their other senses are diminished. If you overdo it with the makeup, you're going to spend half of your career defending yourself. As a woman, I do understand the pressures to look good in a beauty-obsessed world, but we must remember that we are apart from the world and not a part of it. At the same time, if you can, do glamour photo sessions, but when you're on stage, you should always keep the focus off yourself and on the Word of God. If you end up putting on too much makeup before your shows, the number of people whom you can minister to will begin to diminish because people often believe what they see before they're willing to believe what they hear. You may say in your heart that you don't care what others say or think, but if being modest in your appearance could draw more souls to the God in you, why would you lose that opportunity for the sake of your pride? I'm not saying that you ought to refrain from wearing makeup or being fashionable; I'm actually saying the opposite. What I am encouraging you to do is to be mindful of your appearance so that you don't end up being a distraction or a deterrent to the people God may send your way.

Your Armor

As with all things, do not forget to put on the full armor of God wherever you go. You have to ask God to keep you because you cannot keep yourself. Temptation will be lurking in every corner that you pass by, and it's so easy to fall into it, especially when you're going through the storms of life. What is the full armor of God?

Ephesians 6:11-18 (NIV): Put on the full armor of God, so that you can take your stand against the devil's schemes. For our struggle is not against flesh and blood, but against the rulers, against the authorities, against the powers of this dark world, and against the spiritual forces of evil in the heavenly realms. Therefore, put on the full armor of God, so that when the day of evil comes, you may be able to stand your ground, and after you have done everything, to stand. Stand firm then, with the belt of truth buckled around your waist, with the breastplate of righteousness in place, and with your feet fitted with the readiness that comes from the gospel of peace. In addition to all this, take up the shield of faith, with which you can extinguish all the flaming arrows of the evil one. Take the helmet of salvation and the sword of the Spirit, which is the word of God. And pray in the Spirit on all occasions with all kinds of prayers and requests. With this in mind, be alert and always keep on praying for all the Lord's people.

Anytime you go in the midst of God's people, you're going to find yourself in the midst of the devils who are assigned to distract and destroy God's people, so always take God with and in you wherever you go. Wear holiness as your garment, for holiness is the beauty of God's glory, and it blinds the natural senses of men, causing them to see the glory of God. One difference you'll notice between an Artist who ushers in the glory of God versus an Artist who gives a good performance is the crowd's response. When an Artist draws souls to God, people remember the experience itself. They'll often talk about how God showed up, and they'll talk about the deliverance that took place during that Artists' performance. When an Artist draws attention to themselves, people see them as nothing but entertainers, and they'll talk about how good (or bad) of a show that Artist put on. Nevertheless, the people will always invite back and remember the Artist who brought God in their presence.

Your Online Image

One thing that we often forget is that people are visual creatures first, and in many cases, we'll only get one chance to win a person over or encourage them. Sometimes, first impressions are all we get, but the pride that's entered so many leaders of today has caused them to stiffen their necks and not care about the souls that are being lost because of their appearances. We can't lie to ourselves and say that we won't be held accountable for every soul who slips through our fingers. We've got to make sure that our images draw people to God as much as our words draw them to Him. If our mouths are saying one thing, while our images are saying another, we'll lose many of the souls God sends our way because, again, people are visual creatures.

One of the atrocities I've witnessed on social media is the men and women who claim to be evangelists, teachers, prophets, pastors, and apostles...people who are nothing more than parades of flesh used by the devil to draw the hearts of men and women after themselves. It's no wonder that the church is getting a bad reputation in today's (revamped) version of church. For example, I've noticed a lot of women who are scantily clad, seductive, and immoral. I've seen women showing off their derrieres or their cleavage, all the while, tagging God's name to their photos, and this is nothing more than a mockery of the true gospel of Jesus Christ. Many Christian men display photos of themselves half naked, and even though men aren't exactly infamous for showing off their bodies, many believing men promote sexuality on their social media profiles. They will often post pictures of half naked women, or show off pictures of themselves doing worldly things like drinking or reveling.

What many leaders don't realize is people are watching them to see if they practice what they preach, and many of the people who follow

their ministries aren't doing so with the intent
of exposing them. They're doing this because
they've come across many worldly Christian
leaders, and they want to prove to themselves
that there are some men and women after
God's own heart who are still in the pulpits.
When they see us dressing provocatively,
swearing, sharing lewd photos online, or being
hateful, many people lose hope in the church
and return to the world. This was
undoubtedly Satan's plan. He has learned to
use the church to repel the world, rather than
drawing them, and he does this by perverting
the minds of many of today's leaders. He
perverts their minds by causing them to seek
the things of this world, rather than seeking to
draw souls to the Lord. Once they start
looking at the world and all it has to offer, they
begin to follow in Eve's footsteps before she
fell. Remember, Eve considered the fruit that
the serpent tempted her to eat, meaning, she
stared at that fruit and meditated on what the
enemy told her for too long. The same goes for
today's' church. The fruit that Satan offers the
church today is the wealth of this world, and

the fame that comes with it. If we stare at the world and all it has to offer for too long, we'll begin to consider the enemy's offer, and it won't be long before we've fallen into temptation and stumbled into sin.

Your online presence is just as important as your physical appearance. As a matter of fact, you'll find that you're going to reach more people online than you do locally. That's because the Internet reaches the entire world, but physically, you can only be in one place at a time. The problem with many of today's Christian Artists is they don't know or understand the importance of professionally branding their ministries, so they throw together websites and refuse to invest in their ministries. Now, while the church is busy being too cheap to invest in their ministries, the people of the world are spending their last to invest in their music. What this tells us is that there are more people in the world who believe in themselves than there are people in the church who believe in God.

What I witnessed when I worked with the world was the tenacity of many of the secular Artists. They invested in their brands, they called around, and they would not take "no" for an answer. Even though many of them didn't garner the fame they'd wanted, they still made enough money to feed their families.

Your online image should be professional, clean, and eye-catching because many of the people who stumble upon your website, or one of your online profiles, will be people who've never heard of you. If your website or branding says that you're a struggling Christian Artist who's too cheap to invest in the music you're trying to sell them, they'll leave your site, forget your name, and invest in other Artists who believe in what they're trying to sell. This means if you have low-budget branding, you're going to lose more people than you draw. As a matter of fact, it's better to have no branding at all than to have low-budget looking branding.

A lot of Artists are struggling financially, but

your followers should never know that. If your followers think you are struggling to make ends meet, they won't take you seriously. If they think you're a successful Artist who sells a lot of CDs, they'll want to invest in you because they'll think that everyone else is investing in you. If your music is good to them, they'll tell their friends and loved ones about it. Sure, many of your listeners will bluetooth or email your songs to their friends and families, and even though this is frustrating, please keep in mind that your audience is growing. You should always include a disclaimer on your CDs and have a disclaimer available for those looking to purchase your Mp3 files, but there will always be some people who will ignore the disclaimer and share your music with everyone they know. If you spend too much time worrying about them, you'll lose focus on the bigger picture.

People believe what they see. If your online branding looks bland, they'll think your music is bland. That's why you should always hire professional or Godly-gifted web designers and brand managers. Make sure your website, flyers, and your photographs are professional, high quality, and up-to-date with today's web standards. Do not attempt to build your website yourself if you have no web design training. I've actually come across many Christian Artists whose music was written and performed in pure excellence, only to view their online branding and realize that they don't believe in themselves. Of course, I can see their potential, just like everyone else can see their potential, but they obviously can't see it for themselves.   For this reason, I've overlooked featuring many Artists in the magazine I run because I often link back to those Artists, and I don't want to promote anything that's less than excellent. At the same time, I want to discourage this low-budget trend that's become the craze of so many Christian Artists. God told me to display excellence in everything He's given me to do, so if I have to abide by those standards, it's only right that the people I affiliate myself or my brand with also follow those standards. Believe it or not, this is the mindset of many

43

Christian leaders and promoters today. If you don't believe in your gifting enough to invest fully in it, no one else is going to believe in it for you. You'll have a bunch of opportunists coming your way, promising to promote and develop you as an Artist, but when you're dealing with the music industry, you're going to end up dealing with many shady people who see you as an opportunity to promote themselves and earn some extra cash. The reality is that opportunists often see the potential in the Artists they pursue, but they also see that the Artists don't realize their own potential. Of course, this is easily determined when viewing your online branding and how you carry or feature yourself as an Artist.

When I worked with the secular world, I was working with one Artist whose career seemed to be budding fast, but he was impatient and would not invest in his brand. He looked for others to do the investing in him. He'd been looked at by a few major record labels, but they'd passed him by when they noticed that he wasn't investing in himself. He surrounded

himself with many opportunists who could see
the potential of his music, and he waited
impatiently for someone else to get him to
where he wanted to be. One of the labels
who'd looked at him said that he needed to get
his website views up. They didn't want to
invest in someone who hadn't already made a
name for themselves. Opportunity behind
opportunity passed him by, but many
opportunists flocked to him.

One guy in particular promised the Artist that
he could get him the fame he wanted. He'd
said that he had some major connections in the
music industry, and the Artist was all-too-eager
to work with him. After a while, it became
evident that the man didn't have the
connections he claimed to have, and he'd
focused most of his attention on getting my
attention. When he realized that I wasn't
interested in him, he began to show his true
self. He then used the Artist's identification
and went and got things on credit in the
Artist's name. How did this happen? The
Artist believed in himself, but not enough to

invest in himself. When you're having to depend on other people's money, you are giving those people power over your ministry; you are giving them the ability to determine if you'll succeed or fail. That's too much power to put in man's hands.

I ran across a Christian Artist when I first started branding the church, and I can remember that her music was too good not to be heard by the world. Her songs, her presence, and her style were all so well put together that I was sure she'd made and sold thousands, if not, millions of CDs. I thought I was just out of the loop and hadn't heard of her, so I started searching online for her website and other branding, but they didn't exist. I was shocked to see that a woman with such a powerful anointing hadn't invested in that anointing; after all, she had an album or two selling online, and she was doing concerts, but she'd neglected one of the most important tools in today's marketing arena: her online presence. And she wasn't the only one. I ran across another young lady who'd sold many

CDs and had many professional music videos online, but she didn't have a website. This is common with Christian Artists because the general mindset is that Christian music isn't all that popular, but this isn't true. Sure, if you compare our YouTube video views with a secular Artist's YouTube video views, you'll notice that the world comes out in millions to support their own, whereas, many in the church are not supporting their own. Instead, they're casting their votes with the world, viewing and paying for the secular Artist's music, all the while, criticizing Christian Artists for selling or promoting their music. Please understand that people like this aren't Christians who love secular music; they are secular people who think the church owes them something. They don't support the church because they're not a part of the church; they only go to the building and learn the lingo. Nevertheless, you've got to brand your online image as if you're expecting billions of people to view your website and online profiles immediately. This means don't go in with the attitude that you'll throw something

together today, and get the site redesigned
tomorrow. Have it designed as if you're
expecting a major showcasing of the site today
because you don't know when success will call
your name.

Photography

Photography is an important part of your branding, and should not be overlooked. The people who hear your music will want to see your face because, again, people are visual creatures, and there's no way to get around that.

When hiring a Photographer to take your photos, be sure to follow the tips below:

1. Check out the Photographer's portfolio. If the Photographer's portfolio displays any images that you wouldn't be comfortable sharing at church, don't work with that Photographer. The reason is there are many people in the church struggling to overcome lust, for example, and if you're at an event and decide to show them your photos, you may have to flip through a bunch of lewd photos to get to your own. Hire family or portrait Photographers,

preferably Christian Photographers who
live and abide by the same moral code
as yourself.

2. Always take someone with you to the
photo shoot, especially if you've met the
Photographer online.

3. Studio sessions on a white background
are always preferred by web designers
because they easily can cut you out of
that background and place your image
on your website.

4. If your session will be in front of a white
background, be sure to wear clothing
that makes it easier for your Graphic
Designer to cut your photo out.
Mention to the Photographer that many
of the images will be cut out and
displayed on your website. Most
Photographers are Graphic Designers,
and they'll know what to do from there.
If your website will have a white
background, it's okay to wear all white
and take your photos in front of a white
background since your Graphic
Designer won't have to cut your photos

out.

5. Before choosing a Photographer, view at least twenty different Photographers and their portfolios. The reason is some Photographers don't have professional equipment, and after you've seen the portfolios of several Photographers, it'll be easier to tell the difference between the good ones and the not-so-good ones. Work with Photographers who are passionate about their trades. Their passion will be evident in their portfolios.

6. Don't be cheap. Cheap people compromise easily, and their branding suffers as a result. Before I became a Photographer, I went online to find Photographers in my area. This was during a time when my mind was still being renewed, and I was cheap. I wanted a studio session with a white background, but I didn't want to pay the three hundred bucks that most folks with studios asked for, so I started looking at on-location Photographers.

I'd prayed and asked the Lord to send me to the Photographer He wanted me to work with, and I noticed that He kept sending me back to a local Christian Photographer who did studio sessions for over three hundred dollars. I'd made up my mind that I didn't want to pay anything over $150, so I kept looking for someone else to work with, nevertheless, almost every other link I'd clicked belonged to him. Finally, I gave in and went where God wanted me to go, and I've never regretted it.

7. Take several outfits with you to the session, and be prepared to change clothes.

8. If you have a friend or family member who normally does your makeup, bring them with you, as you'll need to have your makeup refreshed or changed once you've changed clothes.

9. Before you start the session or immediately upon starting the session, ask the Photographer to take about five photos of you, and then, show you those

photos. The reason is that sometimes, we may not like the way our hair or makeup looks on camera, so if you get to see this at the start of the shoot, you can make the necessary changes. That way, you don't end up with a bunch of photos that you're too ashamed to display.

10. Utilize Google and look for posing suggestions before you go to your session. All too often, people show up expecting the Photographer to tell them how to pose, and most Photographers can only give you a few posing ideas, but after ten or twenty minutes, the Photographer expects you to be creative.

11. Make sure to ask for your images on CD before starting the session. Your Graphic Designer will need the digital images and not the prints.

12. Ladies, if you're going to do your own makeup, make sure you're good at applying your makeup. It's not the Photographer's fault if you don't like your own face, nor is the Photographer

obligated to go outside of the agreed upon time-frame to ensure you walk away happy. The Photographer's job is to take your photos, and once they've done this, they've fulfilled their end of the agreement. Watch some YouTube videos and practice applying your makeup. After you've applied the makeup, take pictures of yourself. Your Photographer is not going to reschedule the photo shoot at the last minute, so make sure you are ready before you go to the session.

13. Fellows, avoid using new barbers before coming to a photo session because you don't know if you'll like how they cut your hair. Use barbers whose work you are familiar with and comfortable with. If you use a new barber, make sure you've viewed his portfolio before you go to him. Your Photographer is not going to reschedule the photo shoot at the last minute, so make sure you are ready before you go to the session.

14. If you've got oily skin, take an astringent

with you, along with some cotton swabs or towels. Ask the Photographer to tell you if your skin looks oily on any of the photos. Most Photographers look through their camera's stills to see how they're doing, but many of them won't tell you if your face is too oily or your hair is out of place. It's always good to ask the Photographer to mention these things before the start of the session.

15. Ladies, the best hairdos to wear to a photo shoot are the ones that are changeable. If you can pull your hair up for some photos, and let it hang down for other photos, you'll like more of your photos than if you come with a hairdo that can't be changed.

16. Fellows, it's okay to smile in your photos. The general mindset of most men is smiling makes them look feminine, and this is not true. You don't have to frown or look emotionless on your photos. Instead, practice your smile at home, and if you want to avoid looking feminine, simply avoid wearing

colored or glossy lip gloss to the session.

17. Fellows, it's okay to wear powdered foundation (for the session only), especially if your skin is less than perfect. Just make sure that you go to a cosmetologist who can perfectly match a foundation to your skin. Also, be sure to put the foundation on after you've put your clothes on; that way, you won't get the foundation on your clothes. Wear a jacket or some type of covering over your clothes before applying the foundation. When I went to the photo session I mentioned earlier, I'd taken my then-husband with me, and his skin was badly discolored. He had dark spots on his face and around his eyes, so I'd convinced him to let me put my foundation on him, seeing, as it were, that we were the same complexion. After he started seeing his photos, his confidence went through the roof, and he loved every one of those photos. Of course, you can't tell he's wearing foundation, and that's the point.

18. It's always good to know beforehand what colors work well with your complexion.

19. If you want to look slimmer, wear dark clothes and avoid horizontal stripes. If you want to appear taller, avoid wearing long shirts or baggy pants.

20. Confident people take better photos. As a Photographer, I absolutely hate to work with insecure clients because the way they contort their faces usually reflects their insecurities. Insecure people won't give the Photographer their best smiles, nor are they willing to venture outside of their insecurities to embrace new poses. Insecure people almost always end up not liking their photos and blaming the Photographer. The ones who blame themselves often say things like, "I'm not very photogenic," when they are. The issue is they're insecure and fearful. I remember doing a session with an insecure woman, and trying to get her to come outside of her shell. She wouldn't.

She just kept going to the different spots at the location we were at, standing the same way she'd stood in the previous photos, and offering up the same faint smile she'd given me in the previous photos. Needless to say, she wasn't crazy about her photos and neither was I. Every other photo session I'd done that day with different clients had been perfect because my other clients showed up wearing their personalities, and it radiated through their photos. Don't be scared of your own beauty. After all, you'll be able to look through the photos once they're done and delete what you don't like. People who are unattractive (by the world's standards), but are confident take better photos than people who are attractive (by the world's standards), but are insecure.

One of the challenges many Photographers face is uniformed clients who come to the session expecting the camera to make them look the way they want to look. The camera will only record what it sees, and for this reason, you should educate yourself before the session. Make sure you are comfortable in your own skin, and don't go to the session expecting the Photographer to work miracles on your self esteem. Tell yourself that you're beautiful and take a few photos of yourself practicing your smile.

Finding Inexpensive Photography
If you can't afford a professional Photographer, there are some things you can do to get the photos you need to start your branding. Honestly, I hate saying "If you can't afford a professional Photographer" because most people can afford them, it's just that they are accustomed to investing their money in other directions, so they tell themselves that they can't afford a Photographer when they can. Helping people to find their way around professionalism is not my forte, but the reality is...some people are just plain cheap and they are not going to spend their money branding their ministries. The sad part is their ministries won't grow because they refuse to sow seeds

into those ministries. They look for others to sow seeds into their ministries, thus, giving the wrong people power over their ministries. Below are a few tips to getting your photos taken inexpensively.

1. **Buy a professional camera.** Now, I know what you're saying...buying a professional camera costs way more than hiring a Photographer, and this is partly true. You can purchase a good, high-resolution, professional camera for around $500 or more. The average in studio Photographer is going to charge you over $300 to take photos in their studios, and around $150-$250 to take photos outside the studio. If you buy your own camera, you can save yourself thousands of dollars because think of it this way: After you've hired an in-studio Photographer twice, you've probably paid for his camera. You'll spend more than you want to spend initially, but you'll save money in the future; plus, you'll have the ability to take photos anytime you want to take them. If you

want the in-studio look, you can buy a backdrop and lighting for around $300. If you don't have the room for a backdrop, you can buy a portable backdrop that folds, and you can take that backdrop outside during daylight hours and have one of your friends take your photos. A portable backdrop is around $150, and it's a great resource to have.

2. **Find your Photographer on Craigslist**, but remember, take someone to the session with you, and don't meet the Photographer in secluded places. You'll find many local Photographers on Craigslist, looking to build their portfolios, and some of them will do your sessions for little or nothing. Remember, ask questions about the type of photography they're into, and make sure to only work with family and portrait Photographers.

3. **Call some of the local universities and colleges that offer photography classes.** Many schools allow their students to

earn some of their grades by taking photos of the people who volunteer to have their photos taken. Ask around and be sure to mention that you'll promote the Photographer's work at any events you go to.

4. **You can do it yourself, even though I advise against it.** In the original book, *The Gospel Propeller*, I advised Artists to get inexpensive digital cameras and take photos of themselves in front of white sheets. *(Yeah, I didn't know any better).* Nevertheless, even though I would recommend against this now, I do say that it's better than holding up your cell phone and taking photos of yourself. I've had many more years of experience branding ministries and ministers now, and I'm never too happy to see unprofessional photos being sent my way because they take away from the websites, flyers, and any other branding the Artist has. For this reason, I avoid working with people with low-budget thinking.

5. **Search for local Photographers on social media**, and see if you can barter services with them. To barter, you must have something to offer them that is of equal or greater service than what you're looking to get from them. Promises to pay the Photographer off once you've "made it big" will not only offend the Photographer, but it may give your ministry a bad name.

Always remember to respect the gifts and businesses of others, and don't run around looking to get everything free. Again, it is better to pay a Photographer, but if you absolutely, without a question or a doubt, cannot afford a Photographer, then you can consider the aforementioned list.

Building Your Brand

Building your brand is just as important as the songs you sing, nevertheless brand building is one of the most overlooked steps in ministry development. All too often, Artists will put off branding their ministries because they don't want to make the financial sacrifices they'll have to make to do so. As a brand developer, one of the situations I'm commonly faced with is having to tell another leader that I don't work freely. Nowadays, I don't have to have that conversation as much as I did when I hadn't properly branded my company, but I still get people who call me and ask for free services. One of the most common promises people say to me is: "I know my ministry is going to go to new heights, and if you'll just help me out, I promise you that when I make it big, I'm going to bless your socks off." Of course, I have to decline their offers because, first and foremost, ministry isn't about "making it big", and secondly, God ministered to me about this mindset before. He said to me that everyone who He's gifted for success is provided the seeds they'll need to acquire that success, but the problem is, most people cover themselves in their seed. I remember ministering this to a girl who was asking me if I would publish her book freely, and in return, she said that once she'd earned the money back from her book, she'd "bless me real good." Of course, I knew better and I know that the mindset she was operating in is a mindset of poverty. I told her that if God gave her the book to write, He would give her the provision to write and publish that book. We hung up the line with her saying that she was going to pray for provision.

A few days later, I'd logged into Facebook and noticed that she'd published a post, telling everyone that she'd just gotten a lump sum check in the mail. She wasn't expecting the check, and she posted up that she'd gotten her hair done, took her kids to a theme park, and pretty much, blew away the money. I didn't respond to her, I just shook my head and kept on scrolling. A few weeks later, that same woman was back in my inbox asking me again if I'd be willing to publish her book for free, or to give her a discount, and I said no. This mindset is very common with a lot of believers because a lot of folks get saved, but they refuse to sit still long enough so that God could renew their minds.

After working with so many low-budget thinking believers, I finally made up my mind to screen the people I worked with because people who have a wrongful relationship with their money are oftentimes difficult to work with. First off, people with poverty mindsets will often try to get work done freely, and when this doesn't work and they actually pay someone to do the work for them, they usually want more than they've paid for. Anytime I've worked with leaders who have mastered their finances, rather than being mastered by their finances, I've noticed that they are easy to work with. They simply want excellence and they know that they've got to honor God's people by paying them. People with low-budget thinking don't care to honor anyone; they're too busy trying to hold on to the money they've come to love and idolize so much, and that's why money evades them.

Building your brand has to be a careful process, and should not be rushed. If you can't afford to hire a professional Photographer and have your website professionally designed at the same time, the best thing to do is hire the Photographer for now. You can always go back and hire the Web Designer once you've gotten more funds. Becoming anxious and building your own site will only reflect poorly on your ministry. All the same, hiring a professional Web Designer, and sending them a bunch of unprofessional photos you've taken with your cell phone will also reflect poorly on your ministry.

There was a time when I accepted every Christian web design order that came my way. I'd gotten hired by some guy to build his ministry's website, and at first, I was excited about working with him. That was...until he sent me the photos he wanted on his site. I did for him like I'd done for so many people before him...I offered to help him find a local Photographer who would take some professional photographs of him at a reasonable rate, but he refused. He just wanted the website up. I pride myself in designing excellent, star-quality websites, so having to work with a bunch of blurry, low-quality photos was mental torture for me. Additionally, like most people with low-budget thinking, he wanted to get the most work done for the least bit of money. Working with him was an experience I loathed with every fiber of my being. That's because he was unteachable; plus, I knew his photos would take away from the quality website I was going to design for him.

On another occasion, I'd gotten hired by a woman who wanted me to design her website, but she'd sent me some really blotchy and blurry photos. I reached out to her and asked her if she'd go to a Photographer in her area if I found one that was reasonably priced. She agreed. I looked on Craigslist.com and found a Photographer in her area. He was Christian, he had his own studio, his sessions were reasonably priced, and his work was beyond excellent. She went to the Photographer, and her photos were breathtakingly phenomenal. I designed her website, and everything came out to perfection. That's because she had a teachable spirit, and she wasn't more into her money than she was into her brand. Her site and her entire brand radiated with excellence, and of course, people are drawn to beautiful things. Your brand is important, and there's no way to get around that fact.

The first five things you need to build your brand is:
1. Your website.
2. Professional photos.
3. A professionally written bio.
4. Professionally written, produced, and mastered music.
5. Your ministry plan.

That's why you have to surround yourself with

the people you need the most, but make sure you are paying them or bartering with them.

Your Website
Your website should be professionally designed, and your domain name should be your name or the name of your ministry; for example, if your name is Jason Laxbacker, your domain would be JasonLaxbacker.com or whatever your ministry's name is. Whenever using domain names, always try to find the simplest and easiest domain to remember because a lot of people aren't great spellers. If your ministry's name is Anointed For Praise and Worship Ministries, you should not buy www.AnointedForPraiseAndWorshipMinistries.com as no one will remember this. Instead, the easiest way to shorten this domain is to look at the first letter of every word and use it. For example, afpwm.com or a4pawm.com would be great domain names for this ministry. You can even make it easier to remember by just having a4praise.com

When you find a domain name, go ahead and

buy it. Please know that there are people out there whose sole source of income is buying and reselling the domains they know other people want. I helped a guy to search for a domain for his website one evening, and I stumbled upon a domain that would normally be considered a premium domain. I urged him to get the domain name, and I told him that it was a premium domain listing that had not been caught yet. I could tell that he wasn't sure about the domain, but I assumed that he'd gotten it anyway. A few days later, I received a call from the guy, telling me that someone else had purchased his domain name. I wasn't surprised, and I told him that I knew it would be gone if he hadn't went ahead and purchased the domain. He later got another domain that wasn't nearly as good as the one he'd found initially.

When you come across a good domain, go ahead and buy it. If it's a premium domain, buy it up for a few years to ensure that you don't lose it. Another friend of mine didn't have her domain on auto renew, and her domain ended up expiring. A woman commonly known for buying expired domain names purchased her domain and tried to sell it back to her for over $500. Again, there are people out there whose sole source of income is buying and selling domains. The woman who'd purchased my friend's domain was infamous and largely abhorred because of her practices, and many people had posted reviews and written articles about that woman. Of course, I told my friend to go ahead and get a different domain name since her domain wasn't a premium domain nor did she have a lot of traffic coming to that domain. I knew that once the domain had expired, the woman would release it because she's not earning from it, and that's what she did. A year later, the lady released the domain and my friend was able to buy it again, but this time, she took my advice and bought it up for a few years to ensure that she didn't lose it again.

When searching for a Web Designer, it is always better for you to get your own domain, rather than allowing the Designer to get it for you. Many Designers register the domains in their own names to ensure that their clients don't go to other Designers, since Web Design is an unstable business. They not only register the domains in their names, but many Designers will charge you a lot of money to release your domain to you. I've even seen cases where the Designers refused to release the domains altogether because they were upset that their clients had decided to go with another Designer. It is always good for you to get the domain yourself and register it in your name under your own account. You can then give the Designer the password to your account to point your domain to the site they've designed for you. This way, if you should decide to go with a different Designer in the near future, you can simply point your domain to your new site without having to reason with your old Designer.

When searching for a Web Designer, also be sure to check out the Designer's portfolio and look for any online reviews that may be posted about that Designer. The reality is there are some Designers out there who don't operate by the same moral code as others, and they can be pretty demanding when it comes to their work.

Before you hire a Designer, make sure you have the information for your website ready. Remember, Web Designers take what you have and publish it. They don't create the content for you; that's an entirely different service with an entirely different fee. Additionally, make sure you have enough information to fill the number of pages you are hiring the Designer to create for you. As a Web Designer (yes, I wear many hats), one of the common mishaps I run into is people ordering, for example, five page websites when they only need three pages. The issue is they've seen someone else with a five page site, so they decided that they needed five pages. As a result, many people have pretty extended, but empty, websites. Of course, I tell my clients the truth and let them know the amount of pages they actually need, but if they insist on getting more than what they need, I have to comply with their requests.

Another pet peeve of mine (as well as other Designers) is a client who likes another Designer's work, but don't want to pay the price required to hire the other Designer. So, what the client does is hire a Designer who fits into their budget, but then, tries to get that Designer to design like the Designer they didn't want to pay. Please know that every Designer has his or her own style of Design, and that's why it's important to view the Designer's portfolio, and it's also important to pay the Designer you actually want. One thing I've seen more than fifty percent of Designers do who were faced with these type of clients is to start ignoring those clients. They'll do the work, and if the client requests a revision or do-over, the Designer ignores them. I've had many, many people come to me complaining about their Web Designers, and I'm always honest with them. You can't go into McDonald's and tell them to make their burgers like Burger King's. It's an insult, and you have to understand that the Web Designer cannot and will not work on a project for months that would normally take them a couple of weeks or days to complete. If you're a difficult client, you're going to find yourself being ignored, or even blocked, by your Web Designer, and there's nothing you can do about it because Web Design is a service. This means you can't ask for a refund and if you apply for a refund through Paypal or your credit card company, you will lose since services aren't covered under payment protection. Hire the Designer you want to work with, rather than hiring the one you can afford to work with. If you go with the Designer you can afford, it's okay to send them links to a few sites that you like to give them an idea of what you want, but please understand that the Designer will design the site according to his or her own style. They may pinch a few ideas from the sites you've shown them, but the end result will be a site put together in their own style. I had a client hire me to design two sites for him, and working with him was nothing short of a Designer's nightmare. He had already saw another Designer's work, and he'd made up in his mind that he liked the other Designer's style. He didn't take time out to review my work because if he'd done so, he would have seen that I was more advanced of a Designer than the guy he was coveting.

Anyhow, the client sent me a website and told me that he wanted me to design his site exactly like that site. I was disgusted because the site he'd sent to me was not an attractive site; it was outdated, and it was obvious that the Designer of that site didn't have much design experience. I tried to reason with the client, but he was insistent. Once I put the first rendition of the site together, he looked at the site and didn't like it because I'd applied my style to the site to make it look better. He wasn't happy with his site until I revised it and made it as ugly as the other site. After that awful experienced, I stopped working with people who wanted my fees but another Designer's style. Nowadays, I tell my clients that each Designer has his or her own style, and to be sure they like my style before hiring me. I've had many new web designers come to me, complaining that their clients had told them to design their sites the same way I designed my sites. Of course, these women were charging a lot less than I was because they didn't have the experience or the portfolio I had. A lot of people don't realize that such requests make a Web Designer's job a nightmare because they're not allowed to be as creative and gifted as God has designed them to be, but they're instead expected to tap into another Designer's gifting, and this is impossible. When you give a Web Designer a hard time, that Designer will likely respond by delaying the design process and ignoring your calls.

When sending in photos of products such as your CD covers, be sure to send in high-resolution, professionally designed images. You'd be amazed at how much an unprofessional image could affect your website.

Professional Photos
You can find professional Photographers online, but make sure you're in agreement with their portfolio and the quality of the photos

they've taken previously. Don't settle for a Photographer just because they're within your price range. It is better to pay the one who can give you what you really want than to settle for another Photographer.

If you can find a Photographer you can retain for future shoots, that Photographer would be better suited for you. Photographers love to work with talented people because those people bring more exposure to their portfolios than normal, everyday people. Many Photographers will even barter with talented people if they think they can get more exposure to their work, but the worst thing you can do is show off their work without giving them credit.

Your Biography
Hire professional writers to write your biography, and make sure that it's in third person. Also, if you haven't done much of anything yet, forgo the bio for now, and just focus on having a site that displays what you have done. Don't send in lengthy bios talking

about your family life. A bio should talk about your professional life, but it can include snippets from your personal life, as long as the information ties into your profession.

Your Team
Your team should include your Manager, Music Producer, Booking Agent, your label or Music Distributor, Videographer, Publisher, your Beat-Maker, your Songwriter (if you don't write the songs yourself), and your Audio Engineer. Building a great team is essential to the success of any and every Artist. Additionally, you need your Web Designer, Graphic Designer, and Photographer.

Don't be so eager to get your music out there without first looking into building a team. Sometimes, the team will come along after you've started doing a lot of the work yourself and they see that you are serious about your ministry, but you at least need to have your website, photos, and some music on hand.

Your Ministry Plan

Most Artists don't realize the importance of having a business plan, so they pretty much leave their ministries in the hands of the people who believe in them more than they believe in themselves. This is a mistake that will almost always cause you to place your ministry and music in the hands of industry vultures, opportunists who are more interested in lining their pockets than they are in helping you get your ministry off the ground. You've got to believe in what God has given you, and please understand that you won't be a professional at everything overnight. It takes time, dedication, and persistence to build a great Artist.

Surround yourself with people who believe in the gifts God has given you, but more than that, people who believe in God, Himself. Sit down with those people and try to develop a ministry plan (the equivalent of a business plan). Make sure your ministry's plan stretches up to ten years, detailing your plans for each year; that way, you have something to strive for, rather than just leaving your ministry to chance.

Building Your Brand

When building your brand, never allow your branding to be inferior to anyone else's branding, including celebrities. Remember, your music can be great, but if your branding doesn't match the quality of your music (or vice versa), you won't go very far with your gifting. Work with the best of the best, and always make sure that God is glorified in everything you do. You are representing Him, so let your branding be Kingdom quality.

Marketing Your Music

Recording the music is easy, but marketing your music is the real challenge. You've done the hard work. You've written and recorded the songs; you've had your music mixed and mastered, and you've had your music professionally packed. Now, it's time to market your music, but you don't know where to start. The best place to start is locally, and here's why. When I worked with secular Artists, I'd spoken with an A & R for a major record label. He'd told me to call him if I'd run across some head-turning talent. I worked with a lot of Artists, but I was sure to avoid calling him about everyone whose music I liked because I wanted him to take me seriously. I wanted him to recognize that if I was calling him, I had someone who transcended the talent I'd come across day to day.

I'd come across a girl whose music was not

only marketable, but her sound and image were superior to most of the Artists I'd come in contact with. I knew the label rep would love her, so I arranged to do a conference call with them both.

Once we'd gotten on the conference call, I was taken aback when the girl confessed that she was already signed to a label. I was upset because I saw the rep as a really good connection, and I didn't want to lose that connection. The rep grabbed his computer, checked out her website, and he loved her music and presentation. It was clear that the label she signed with was doing its job. The A& R wanted to better understand why the Artist wanted to leave her label, so she went on to tell him that the label wasn't getting her the success she wanted fast enough. I grabbed a pen and paper because I knew I was about to learn something new. The rep began asking her how many albums had she sold, and she had impressive numbers. Confused, the rep asked her once again why she was so anxious to get rid of a label that was clearly garnering her some success, and to that she responded that she wanted to go national. Her label had been mainly playing her music locally, so she'd decided that she needed to go with another label. That's when he told her that her label was actually doing their job, and they were doing it well. He said to her what I'd heard another A & R with a different label say. He said that labels aren't too interested in Artists who can't sell themselves locally. He said that an Artist's greatest supporters were the people from that Artist's hometown. Her label was actually setting the foundation for her success the right way. They'd made sure that she was marketable, had a great web presentation, and they were promoting her locally. Even though I was frustrated with her for not telling me that she was already signed, I was thankful for the call because I'd learned a lot about major labels and how they chose Artists. The rep told the Artist to be patient with her label. He told her that he would have loved to sign her if she hadn't been already signed to a label, but at the same time, he didn't believe in trying to undercut the smaller labels, especially when they were doing their jobs.

Your local listeners are the ones who will support you and help bring attention to you from some major labels, if you're looking to be signed to a label. When the people from your hometown and surrounding areas love you, this tells major labels that your music is marketable. Below are ten things I learned by talking with a few A&R reps from major labels:

1. Market yourself locally first. Don't try to jump into the national or international market if you haven't sold yourself locally. Major labels will first look at your local numbers before even considering you.

2. It is better to sell your CDs locally to build your numbers. Don't sell your music for prices that people can refuse. Sell your music locally for cheap, but then, make sure you get the buyers of your music to sign a document stating they've purchased your music. Major labels want to see numbers, and they want evidence that you've sold yourself locally. One of the Artists I worked with sold his CDs for $1 out of the trunk of

his car, and he'd sold 40,000 CDs in a year. He'd also kept records of his sales. This impressed one of the A&R agents I was trying to market him to.

3. Place a tracker on your website so that the label reps can see how many people have visited your site, but make sure you don't reach out to a label until you've gotten your views up. When I sent a rep to an Artist's website, the first thing the rep looked at was the Artist's view count. The Artist's count was too low, so the rep told him to get his numbers up, and then, call him back.

4. Low budget branding hurts an Artist's career more than no branding does. Major labels don't just look at the Artist, they look at everything associated with that Artist. If you've got a do-it-yourself website, a low-budget music video, and an unprofessionally written bio, most, if not all, major labels will pass you by. As a matter of fact, most A&R agents are so busy that they won't spend anymore than a minute on a website if that site is

not up to par.

5. Interviews are good, but be careful who you interview with. Major labels want drama-free Artists who don't have interviews that will eventually come back to haunt them. If you don't have a Manager, call around and set up some interviews for yourself. Make sure you interview with reputable journalists who won't embarrass you on the air.

6. You should never let your name leave the presses. Some Artists get frustrated after a while, and they stop marketing themselves and their music. That's career/ ministry suicide. Even when your albums are not selling, you're not being booked, and people aren't visiting your website, you should continue to keep your face and your music in the media. Set up interviews, keep writing and recording music, and continue to minister publicly so that the people won't forget you.

7. You should always have your own style. One thing labels hate are mock

performers, people who try to look and sound like other Artists. The quickest way to get overlooked is to look or sound like someone else.

8. Always reinvent your brand. People get bored, and so do label reps. If you look and sound the same on all of your albums, the general mindset for a label is you're not versatile and people will quickly become bored with you after you've recorded a couple of albums.

9. Be teachable and surround yourself with teachable people. One Artist I worked with kept losing opportunities because he had a family member managing him who acted as if he knew it all. Many of the people I'd connected with that Artist told me the Artist had major potential, but his manager was a know-it-all who wouldn't take wise counsel. Finally, I'd connected the Artist with a woman who owned her own label, and she told him that if he wanted to get signed to her label or anyone else's label, he'd have to fire his manager.

10. Don't use gospel music as a doorway to launch a career in secular music. For years, many secular artists have put on their church shoes and went into the church looking to launch their secular careers. Even though this method has worked for so many Artists, it is very clear that those Artists did not love nor fear the Lord. Artists who use the church as a platform usually fall from their high places because they dishonored the Lord. If you love the Lord, secular music shouldn't be a genre of music you're looking to get into since secular music promotes a doctrine that goes against the Word of God. If you're singing for the Lord, be faithful and sing for the Lord. If you want to sing for the world, build your platform in the world.

Once your music is professionally written, produced, and distributed, you are ready to market that music to some major Christian labels. Make sure that your online presence is excellent, and that you are engaging with the people who are following your ministry. If you have someone managing your career, of course, you don't have to market yourself, since that would be the Manager's job. But if you're doing it all yourself, please know that a label won't sign you without a Manager, so that's the first thing you need to get out of the way. You can ask an entrusted family member to act as your Manager. When an Artist I was working with was approached by an A&R for a major label, he lost his opportunity when he told the rep he didn't have a Manager. The rep told him to call him once he'd found management, and of course, he called and asked me if I would act as his Manager. Even though I'd agreed to do so, the Artist (and myself) had trouble reaching that rep, and after a dozen calls to him, we finally gave up.

Marketing Your Music to Your Followers

If your music is good and your presentation of that music is good, you will start to have followers. Of course, to get followers, you have to have a presence. You need a presence in your city and surrounding areas, and you need an online presence. The way you present yourself and your music will determine how many followers you have. When you are trying to become a celebrity, this will show in your music, and you will lose the interest of the people because, in ministry, people want something real. They want to follow people who are leading them to Christ and in Christ, not people who are looking to make a name for themselves. So, the most important advice I can give you is make sure you put and keep God ahead of yourself. When you follow God, He will use you to lead His people. When you're following fame and fortune, God will warn His people about you, and your fall will be inevitable should you not repent.

Most people who love Christian and Gospel music are people who have been inspired, encouraged, and changed by the music. What does this mean for you? It means that you should not try to sell yourself to people. They aren't buying your music to see if you "have skills"; they are buying the music because they want to be encouraged, changed, and inspired.

In other words, don't cut God out of the picture and insert yourself in His place. I can't reiterate that message enough because so many Gospel Artists have fallen into the temptations of fame and stardom, and that's why so many people are against Christian Artists promoting their music. If you keep God in the music, and you continue to minister to His people through the music, your music will be as marketable as it is helpful. Here are a few tips to market your music to your followers:

1. First and foremost, you need to determine who your target age group is. A lot of young Artists are coming out creating what is commonly known as Gospel Hip-Hop, and this genre of music doesn't last long in the church because it does not belong in the church. Always remember that music continues to change as our children grow up, and new generations come out with new styles of music. If you want music that transcends the hands of time, stick with Christian or Gospel music. People who

create modern-day music (rap, hip-hop, and the like) end up falling off the charts because the music doesn't change anyone; it simply entertains them. Gospel music was never supposed to be for personal entertainment. Gospel music is supposed to be uplifting, mind-changing, and helpful to a person who's going through one of the many challenges of life. The best age group to market to is the thirty-plus crowd, since the younger crowd tends to mostly follow secular artists. Young folks who love the Lord will be mature enough to buy your music because of their love for God, and their desire to learn more about the Lord. Make sure your music is informative, and make sure that your music is audible.

2. Next, you should always make a big deal out of any albums you have coming out, any videos you're featured in, and any concerts you'll be ministering at. Advertise big, and ask some of your followers to advertise for you. Get

professionally designed flyers, and be sure to offer reward incentives for some of your followers.

3. When on social media, take note of the people who are actively following you, and delete the people who aren't supporting your ministry. You need to do this to make room for new followers. Be engaged with your followers, and have contests where the winners could win a copy of your next album. You can also offer to feature one or more of the winners in your next video shoot.

4. Never use the church as your stage. The sanctuary is not your platform, so don't call around asking leaders if you can come to their churches and perform. Many leaders would consider your request distasteful, and you could earn yourself a bad name. Instead, your gift will make room for you. Just do what God told you to do, and He will open the necessary doors, just as He'll close the wrong doors. Don't question Him, just move with His Spirit. You can,

however, volunteer to perform in local Christian events, but again, it is better to let people come after you than it is for you to go after them.

5. Never compete with other Artists. It's Gospel music, therefore, it's not about you. The message is supposed to help God's people and win souls for Christ. When Christian Artists compete, this gives the church a bad name to go with the bad reputation it's gotten over the years. At the same time, when people see you competing, they are not going to be interested in your music because the spirit you're being led by is not one they want coming through their radios. Remain humble and let your gift make room for you.

6. Call around to some local Christian radio stations and ask what you need to do to get your music featured on their station. Most stations will ask you to mail them a CD, so be sure to do this promptly.

7. Visit some local Christian stores and ask

what you'll need to do to get your CDs stocked on their shelves.

8. Rent a booth at some of the upcoming local events. You can get a listing of upcoming events from your local Chamber of Commerce. Be sure to get a listing of events from the Chamber of Commerce offices in the areas surrounding you as well.

9. Create your own events, and invite some of your city's most renown and beloved leaders to teach and sing at that event. Make sure you plan the event at least twelve months in advance to give people time enough to prepare and to give you time to finance and prepare for the event.

10. Take your music with you everywhere you go. Sometimes, you will be suddenly presented with opportunities and you need to be ready for them. Always have plenty of CDs with you, and always have your business cards on hand as well.

11. Contact as many Christian online radio

shows as possible, and ask if they'll be willing to play your music on their podcast. You'd be amazed at how many people will be excited to promote your music for you.

12. Offer free downloads of one or more of your songs. Find websites that allow you to upload those songs to make them available for free download. Be sure to upload the free downloads to your website as well, requesting people to sign up for your newsletter before being able to access the download. That way, you can send out mass emails, keeping your followers abreast of what's happening with your ministry.

13. Find a reputable email marketer and hire them to send out email blasts for you.

14. Contact some online Christian magazines, and ask if they'll be willing to interview you, feature your music, or offer your free download on their sites. If they're willing to do them all, great! If not, take whatever offer they give you,

and be thankful for it. *P.S. Stay away from low-budget-looking Christian publications.*

15. Have a professional media kit created and distributed.

16. Collaborate with other musicians.

17. Schedule your status updates on social media sites. I know you're too busy to market yourself all the time, but there are programs out there that allow you to schedule your status updates in advance. Utilize one of those programs and create/ schedule your statuses maybe a week in advance.

18. Keep your personal website updated and fresh. That's why it's a great idea to have a Web Designer on your team, and not just a Designer you hire when you need work done. Of course, you'll still have to pay the Designer, but at least, you'll be able to reach them when you need them.

19. Learn to do more than just music. One of the complaints I often hear from musicians is they don't have enough

money to do all of the things or hire all of the people they need on their team. In the meantime, they just sit around and complain about who's not willing to help them. Don't waste your time complaining. Learn to do a lot of the things that need to be done; that way, you will eventually master those crafts. A musician who only knows music is a musician who won't earn a lot.

20. Go where God sends you and don't accept every opportunity that presents itself to you. Some opportunities come from opportunists, and God knows this. That's why you can't cut God out of your ministry. You need Him more than you need a microphone, stage, and an audience. Ask Him to send you where He wants you to go, and if He warns you not to go to a certain place, don't go to that place. Some opportunities will look like great chances to advance yourself, but they are really nothing more than religious brothels designed to bring in and brown down God's people.

> Be led by the Spirit of God and not by
> your flesh.

Finally, there are a few additional promotional
tools you should look into getting and they are:
- Mobile App
- Ringtones
- Google Voice

Make sure that the person or company you
hire to design your mobile app is professional.
One of the keys to marketing your music
successfully is by looking like the success you
want to be. People are drawn to excellence, but
when Artists and other Entrepreneurs go the
do-it-yourself route, or hire non-professionals
to design their apps, they actually do more
damage to their ministries and businesses than
they would have had they just neglected
getting the mobile app altogether. When
people go to your website, they should see
excellence. When they read your newsletters,
they should witness excellence. When they
view your apps, they should see excellence.
They should associate you with excellence in

all things.

As for ringtones, you can use snippets of your music to create ringtones. Make sure the music is mastered and doesn't sound like it was recorded in a garage. You can offer free ringtones as an incentive to get your listeners to sign up for your email list. When they visit your website, a pop-up asking for their email is a good idea when a reward for inserting their email is offered.

And then, there's Google Voice. I absolutely love Google Voice, and I often recommend it to anyone with a business or ministry. Google Voice allows you to get you own free phone number from Google, and you can link that number to your cell phone; that way, when people call the number, it rings your phone. I have one of my business lines through Google Voice, and I have it set up to require the person to say their name before being passed through. This way, I know if a call is personal or professional. My friends and family call my personal line, and like everyone else, I simply answer by greeting them, but when someone calls me on Google Voice, I have to press the number one to answer the call, and I'm able to give my own personalized, professional greeting.

Releasing an Album

Releasing an album is a major event in an Artist's career or ministry, and this event should not be taken lightly. Most major and indie labels launch huge marketing campaigns before the release of an Artist's album, especially if that Artist is considered as one of their huge money-makers. Labels will invest more money in marketing an Artist whose history of sales has proven to be lucrative than they would for an Artist whose history of sales has proven to be unprofitable or an Artist who has no sales history. So, the first order of business for a label is to project the costs associated with the album they are releasing, and then, project how much of a profit they believe they'll earn from that album. But neither a label nor an Artist can forecast how much of a profit they'll make if:

- They don't know the Artist's sale history.
- They don't know the costs associated with the production and distribution of

that Artist's album.

- They haven't launched successful ad campaigns in the past.
- They have not and/or do not intend to invest a lot of money into promoting the album.

For this reason, it is wise for the label and/or the Artist to prepare for the release of an album at least six months to a year ahead of time, and at the same time, it's never a great idea to invest too much into an Artist who doesn't have a sales history to project from. Major labels often invest a fairly decent amount into their newcomers, especially if their newcomers have a decent or lucrative sales history from their album or singles they'd sold before they were signed to that label. That's why major label representatives will always ask Artists about their sales history. They want to know if the Artists are good investments, and if they can expect to see a profitable return on their investments. Labels won't sign Artists if they think they won't make their money back from those Artist's albums, and they won't sign Artists if they suspect they'll only break even from the sales. They want to know that they'll make a huge profit before taking a risk with a person, and that's why major labels often pass up some really talented people who haven't proven themselves. Every investment in an Artist that an album makes is a huge gamble.

What if you're about to release your own album? What should you do to prepare the world and the church for your album's release?

Projecting the Costs

You should always do a cost projection first and foremost. Estimate how many songs you'll have on your album, and how much money you'll spend getting those songs mixed and mastered. Add up the amount of money you'll spend for the packaging and distribution of that album, as well as the marketing campaign for that album. Of course, to do a cost projection, you'll need to know everything you'll need for the creation, production, marketing, and distribution of your album. Of course, to properly market and distribute an album, you will pay a substantial amount of money, but the idea is that you'll make that money back, along with a substantial profit.

To project the costs, be sure to gather your team and conduct the necessary research. How much will your album's artwork cost? How much will the studio charge for your recording time? Of course, you'll have to project studio costs because you won't know how many times you'll have to start over when producing a track. If you have your own studio, it'll be easier to override this cost, and of course, you can release a digital album instead of a pressed album. This would save you a lot of money on distribution costs. How much will you have to pay to package and distribute your album? Always set money aside for unexpected costs, otherwise, your album's release date will likely get set back because of those unforeseen fees.

Don't be in a rush to project your costs. People who do so often spend more money than they anticipated. And don't look for the cheapest routes available. People who do this often spend more than they projected, but the quality of their album is often compromised. Ironically, Artists who try to go the cheap route often end up spending just as much or more than Artists who pay for quality work. All the same, the quality of the cheap Artist's album is reflected in his or her album, and this almost always costs them thousands, if not millions, of sales. Take your time and build a team first, and then, start adding up your cost projections. Once you've estimated how much you need to properly develop, manufacture, package, and distribute your album, you can start the next step.

Projecting Your Profits

Next, you should always have a projection of the profits you believe your album will bring in. To get a better idea of what you should be bringing in, you need to know your target audience, meaning, you need to know the age, gender, race, and economic class of the people who is more likely to buy your album. Oftentimes, Artists discover their target markets by simply releasing album singles, and recording the sales information. If you don't know who you should be marketing to, you'll spend too much money marketing your album to the wrong demographic. A lot of Artists have made this mistake, and this caused their albums to flop. Always make sure you know your target audience before you release an album.

After you've discovered your target audience, the next step is knowing where and how you can reach that audience. What events will you be ministering at, and how many people are expected to attend that event? Information like this is important, and if you're an unsigned Artist, information like this may be hard to acquire, but definitely not impossible. If an event is an annual event, you can call the event's coordinator and ask how many people attended the event the previous year. You can also ask other Artists who've performed or ministered at those events how many people actually bought their albums. For the events that are not annual, your projections should always be based on the amount of seating the building has that the event will be hosted in, and if the event will be hosted outside, consider any other events that were held at that place previously. Also, be sure to consider the weather and any other major events that will be taking place on that day.

You need to know how many people you will have access to, and the percentage of those people who is likely to buy your album. Again, a great way to do this is to release album singles months prior to the release of your album. That way, you'll get a chance to see the demographic and the amount of people who are buying your single; plus, you'll be able to receive listener feedback. Listener feedback is important in helping you to discover which singles should be struck from the album and simply released digitally.

Of course, you need to know your projected costs before you can better estimate your expected profits. Always book yourself at as many shows and events as possible before announcing the release of a new album, so you'll have an audience to announce your album's release to. Telling a bunch of folks on your Facebook page who's never heard your music or saw you perform is about as effective as tapping a stranger on the shoulder at the supermarket and telling them about your new album.

20 Tips to Marketing Your Album's Release

Again, you need to market an album prior to its release six months to a year in advance, but there will be times when you create an album that the Lord will tell you to release almost immediately. Either way, you need to do the cost estimates and profit projections before or while working on the album.

Below, you'll find 20 tips to market your album's release.

1. If you can afford to, hire a Publicist. A Publicist is a person who generates publicity. Check around to see if there are some really good Publicists in your area and if you can afford to work with them. Consider their history of sales before hiring them, and definitely, pray

about them first.

2. Get your album's cover designed and start advertising it online and offline, especially on social media sites.

3. Develop a landing page or website for your new album.

4. Set up one or more interviews to talk about your new album's release.

5. Be sure to get a press release created and distributed. There are many free press release sites that will allow you to upload your press releases.

6. Submit singles to as many radio stations as you can. Get help from the people on your team with distributing the singles if at all possible.

7. Send a few singles to select bloggers and ask them to blog about them. Collect all of the links of the articles and paste them on your website. Make sure you go after bloggers who have substantial amounts of readers. Also, be sure to send the singles to the bloggers months prior to the release of the album or as soon as you can.

8. Create hashtags for your album and post them on social media sites. Get as many of your listeners to post those hashtags as well.

9. Ask your followers to change their middle names on social media to your album's name if at all possible.

10. Set up an album release party and invite as many people as you can.

11. Upload and sell some of your album's singles on streaming sites.

12. Release a few music videos for some of the tracks on your album. Be sure to market your videos so you can get your views up, and make sure your videos are high quality, professional videos.

13. Send out mass email blasts before the release of the album.

14. Find as many local radio station hosts as well as blog radio hosts, and ask them if they'd be willing to interview you on the air.

15. Don't throw away those video bloopers! Post the bloopers on YouTube and other video hosting sites.

16. Be sure to post the lyrics of your singles on your website, as well as other lyric sites. People who learn the words to a song are oftentimes likely to become actual customers than the ones who don't. You can also create a video displaying the lyrics and upload that video to YouTube and other video hosting sites.

17. Get as many people to review your album as possible.

18. Hold contests and give away copies of your album as a reward. Since albums are usually $20 or less, don't make the contests difficult. You can ask people to take pictures of themselves holding up the album's name, and the most creative photos win. You can also have people change their middle names on Facebook to your album's name, and draw the winners' names from a hat via video. Another great idea would be to have graphic artists to create artwork showing their support of your album, and the winner wins a copy of your

117

album, along with a chance to be featured in your next video. Make sure that whatever you are asking of the people, you are giving them something of greater value in return, otherwise, they won't participate.

19. Get your flyers and posters designed, and distribute them everywhere you can.

20. Be sure to get t-shirts and other merchandise created for your album and give some of it away.

Promoting Your Music Locally

One of the first steps to growing your listener count is by promoting your music locally. A lot of Artists take this step for granted, and as a result, they find themselves writing and producing music they cannot sell. Nevertheless, unless you are the town villain, you should always expand your ministry locally before seeking to go national or international.

Below are ten tips to promoting your music locally.

1. Go to the local Chamber of Commerce in your area and your surrounding areas. Get a list of events, and call the event coordinators for some of the events to see what you need to do to minister there. Use wisdom and be prayerful before choosing the events, however.

2. Find out who's writing Christian plays,

and ask if you can minister through music in those plays. Plays are oftentimes musicals, and they are becoming more and more popular. Plus, plays are oftentimes recorded, so your performance *(I hate that word)* will be recorded and distributed, as long as those plays are available.

3. Record your music and try to get people to sing your songs. The more people who sing your music, the more known your music will be. What do people say when they hear a song they like? They often ask, "Who sang that song?" That's because when people hear a song, they want to hear it song by the original Artist. If your song is being sang at events, in churches, and in plays, you'll get more sales. Now, of course, you can restrict the selling and distribution of your song so that no one else can profit from it, but don't be afraid to let someone else sing it. A lot of Artists are competitive and they don't want anyone else to sing their songs, and this

competitiveness does not belong in ministry. As a result, they become their own audiences.

4. Start a contest and let some of the local youth sing your song and record themselves doing it. Let them know that the finalists' videos will be uploaded to your website, and the winner will get rewarded. A great reward would be to let them sing on a track with you on your next album, or, if you have a label, you can say that the winner will be signed to your label. You can also give away material gifts like cash, gift cards, tablet computers, and other gifts people consider valuable. Offering to give away a copy of your next CD is not always a great thing since CDs can usually be purchased for under $20.

5. Stay abreast of any renown Christian Artists who will be ministering in your city or the surrounding areas, and call around to find out what you'd have to do to be an opening act for those Artists.

One of the things many Artists like to boast on is that they were the opening acts for some of today's most celebrated Christian Artists. This is a great boost to an Artist's resume, so don't despise small beginnings.

6. Call the local radio stations and ask what you'd have to do to get your song featured on the radio. If they want money, pay the price if their listener base is worth it. For example, if your city's population is 300,000 people, and one of the local stations airs to 30,000 people, that's ten percent of your city's population. That would be a great station to air your music on. Make sure your music is not inferior to the professionally recorded Artists, otherwise, your first impression may be your last.

7. Include some of your city or town's most beloved people in your music videos. This includes other Christian Artists. Remember, word of mouth is a powerful marketing tool, and when

people hear that the people they love and respect are featured in a music video, they'll tune in. If they like what you've done with the video, they'll share it. *That's why you can't go low-budget and have high expectations.*

8. Enlist the help of some local talents. When I worked with secular artists, I met a young guy who was in school for videography, and he was honestly just as good at what he did as many of the major videographers. A lot of people started taking notice of what he was doing, and they started enlisting (and paying) him to record their music videos. A great music video can even take the sting out of an awful song. Get help from some local talents, and also, go out of your way to promote them. When you look out for others, they will often return the favor.

9. Get the young people involved. Videos that showcase high school students in a popular light have become the craze of YouTube. If you can get some students

(with their parents' permission, of course) to be featured in one of your videos, your listener base will grow dramatically. For example, if there's a lot of crime in your city, write a song that will help unite the city, and get many of the young people involved. Again, you need to have their parents' written permission, and it is never wise to bring the youth in an enclosed environment without other responsible adults being present. Make sure a few of the parents or guardians are present with you every time you record music in an enclosed environment.

10. Give back to your community. Nothing churns the heart of the community more than a local success expressing their love in and around the cities they've grown up in. Even if you come from a small community, never look down on the people you were once a part of. Now, you don't owe them anything but to love them, but always remember that love's arms are never too short to reach

even the smallest person. Artists who
refuse to minister at events, churches, or
cities just because those events,
churches, or cities are small, oftentimes
find themselves being shrunk smaller
than the people they once looked down
on.

Taking Your Ministry International

I've never heard anyone say they didn't want to
go international with their ministries. As a
matter of fact, Jesus was not bound by the four
walls of a traditional church building. Instead,
Jesus went from one land to another
ministering the Word of God to anyone who
would hear the Word. Nowadays, there are so
many people who confine themselves to their
local sanctuaries, not venturing out to let God
use them on a larger scale. A lot of people
want to go international with their ministries,
but are afraid because they're intimidated by
the opinions of traditional church folks. You
see, a lot of people will want to keep your
talent to themselves. There have been cases
where some church leaders had become
offended with one of their church members
because that member had ministered in song
under the roof of somebody else's church. We
know that such behavior is of the flesh, and we
know that God is not for men and women who

seek to confine or limit the limitless gifts He's placed in His people.

First and foremost, before you consider going international, you must branch out from where you are, meaning, you start off locally and branch out until you've reached the national level. People who are anxious to go international, in most cases, are looking to grow their own names, instead of glorifying the Lord to the nations. How does the people in your city and surrounding areas receive you? Have you ventured outside of your state with your ministry? There are 50 states in the United States. How many of those states have you ministered in? Sure, there may be cases where God will open an international door for some people before opening a national door for them, but that's because they allowed God to move according to His will. It may or may not be His will to take you across international waters just yet. You have to ask Him first, and then, wait for His answer. As believers, we often ask God questions, but we don't wait for His answer. Instead, we answer ourselves and move in accordance with our own selfish plans, and when we do this, the Lord has to discipline us. The root word of "discipline" is "disciple", so God makes disciples out of us through His correction.

How does one go international with their song ministry? Below are ten tips to going international.

1. Again, start locally and branch out. When you go international, you want a crowd at home celebrating what God is doing through you. It is the roar of the local folks that is heard throughout the nations, and it is the roar of the nations that is heard across international borders.

2. Study the sound of the nations you want to minister in. Most countries and regions have their own unique sound, and some of those places aren't too welcoming of foreign sounds. To catch their attention, you need to embrace their sound and make music to it. If you're American, one of the great

advantages you have is that most Americans embrace sounds from all nations, often incorporating them in their music. So, you don't have to wait until you're considering Spain, for example, to make Spanish-style gospel music. You can do that at home, and promote that sound locally, and then, nationally before you visit any Spanish countries.

3. Make sure you license your music overseas before marketing your music overseas. If you don't want to license your music overseas, a good alternative to foreign licensing is manufacturing your music in the United States, and then, send your music to distributors in other countries. There are drawbacks to this route, including having to pay the government-imposed tariffs, along with paying the distributor his (or her) fee.

4. Learn the cultures of the people you want to reach out to. Sure, we should never bind ourselves with the traditions and cultures of man, but if you're going

to go before a group of people, you'd better know what they consider offensive. As a matter of fact, you need to know what's offensive to a particular nation before making music that appeals to that nation, otherwise, you may say something in your song that the people consider offensive, or you may do something in your music video that they consider offensive. Educate yourself before trying to go international.

5. A lot of people in foreign nations do love American music, while some people religiously stick with their own sounds. Find out which countries and which people love American music, and then, reach out to some radio stations and ministers in those countries. Ask them if you can send a few CDs to them so that they can promote your music. Don't ask them to sell any CDs for you because some people are very, very poor and you'll never see a dime of that money. Just ask them to play the music

on the radio, and in return, if the music gets a lot of attention in that country or state, you'll be willing to visit the place. *Use safety precautions before visiting other countries, and always stay at one of the local hotels. Never agree to stay in someone's house.*

6. Learn some of the major languages such as Spanish, French, or Portuguese. When you learn to speak and sing in those languages, your ministry will automatically be considered an international ministry. Even though it's better to learn a language itself, you can simply write a song, have it transcribed to another language, and learn to sing that song in the way that the locals of that country would sing it. There is a boy from Brazil, for example, who learned to sing some songs in English, and even though he doesn't speak English, his music is quickly gaining momentum in English-speaking countries.

7. Try to promote your music in mostly

English-speaking countries until you've learned to speak or sing in other languages. *Please know that many of the English-speaking countries have their own style of music, so you still need to learn their sound before attempting to appeal to them.*

8. Collaborate with some international musicians. You'd be amazed at how many Artists in foreign countries would love to work with an American Artist because they want their music playing in America, whereas, you want your music playing in their countries. Collaborate with them, and if you're ever in their countries, you can come together to sing a song you've written. You will also have to sing one they've written so they can place it on their CDs. Agree to market them in America, and have them do the same for you in their countries.

9. Don't limit your audience on social media sites. Reach out to people in foreign lands as well. Be sure to create a

fan page on Facebook, so that you won't be limited to Facebook's 5,000 friend limit on personal pages.

10. Make sure you get a bilingual person on your team, or get an interpreter on your team. This will help you market your music to the nations.

11. Make sure your website is multilingual. You can hire interpreters to interpret your already published English site into other languages. When people come to your site, they should automatically see English (if you're American or in an English-speaking country), but they should also see the options to view the site in their native tongues.

12. Buy the domain extensions for the countries you intend to visit. You can create squeeze pages or blogs, and create a one-page intro to your site. For example, the extension .de is commonly used in Germany. If you want to market your music in Germany, a great idea is that you buy your domain name with the .de extension, and then, attach a blog

page to that domain. Make sure the blog page is in German, and the page links them back to the German-speaking side of your main website.

13. Take over the search engine listings by marketing your site on international blogs and sites. The more sites you're on, the more you'll come up in the major search engines like Google, Bing, and Yahoo.

14. When you have friends, family members, or church members going to other countries, give them a few copies of your CDs, and ask them to give them to some of the local people. Make sure your website's link is on the back of those CDs, or at least have them give out your business card with the CDs.

15. Link up to other Artists who've gone international, and ask them how they did it. New information is almost always useful information.

Also remember that taking your ministry international isn't about selling more CDs and gaining more recognition, it's about evangelizing the nations and winning souls for Christ. This means that you shouldn't just go after the people who can pay for your music. Evangelize the people who need it the most...people who can't give you anything in return for your music. After all, that's what ministry is about. When you reach out to the nations in love, they will extend their arms to you, but again, pray before you go anywhere. I've heard many horror stories of people attempting to go into lands where the people were so against Christianity that they'd thrown rocks and shot at the missionaries. Don't go somewhere just because it's a good idea; always make sure that where you go is a God idea. People who pursue fame often run in circles, but people who pursue the will of God are led by God to the nations. Trust God with all that you do, and make sure that when you go to the nations, God is with you.

Overcoming Opposition

The word opposition is composed of two words: oppose and position. Therefore, opposition is the opposing of one's position. You're going to face opposition, whether you serve the Lord or you serve the enemy. When you serve JEHOVAH, the enemy and this world will oppose you. If you serve the world, you are, in the same, serving the prince of this world, Satan, and the Word of God will oppose you. Wherever you go and whatever you do, you're going to face opposition.

Now, I do understand that some people are looking for nothing but tips on how to grow their ministries, but please know that you're going to face opposition along the way. If you don't know how to deal with opposition, no teacher or book on this earth will be able to help you once you're under attack. You need to know what to do to grow your ministry, but you must also know and understand how to deal with opposition, as well as how to view it.

When I turned away from the secular industry and stopped listening to secular music, I was opposed by the people who were still in the secular industry. I was also opposed by some people in the church who'd pretty much sold out to the idea that they could serve two gods, as long as they did it with a "good heart". Nevertheless, I pressed forward in the Lord, and He blessed me tremendously. When I started working with ministries, I dealt with another kind of opposition because, at that time, I did not know my identity in Christ. I thought that my connections with people would help me to get to where I wanted to be, and because of this mindset, I came across a very wicked woman who referred to herself as a pastor. She offered to help me get my design career off the ground, and she claimed that God had told her that I was an Evangelist. She sent me a certificate in the mail that referred to me as an Evangelist, but God would not allow me to pull that certificate fully out of its envelope. I pulled it out halfway, looked at the text, pushed it back into the envelope, and set it on top of my mother's television set. *I was going through a divorce and living back at my mother's house, so I wasn't in the best place emotionally, and that's why the enemy sent her.* Nevertheless, God kept me, and He used two people I'd met through my business to tell me what type of spirit I was dealing with in that woman. One of the most wicked spirits that loves to come after the people of God is the Jezebel spirit, and that pastor had it. I didn't know how to get away from her, so I just stopped taking her calls. After a ton of calls, threatening voice mails, and condescending emails, she finally got the picture and left me alone...*somewhat.* Over the years, I would get friend requests on Facebook, and the Lord would sometimes warn me that the person sending me the request was that woman. I'd then go to my email address, find her old emails, and put them in the search box on Facebook. Sure enough, it was her going under a different name, but she didn't have sense enough to create a new email. She was opposition manifested, and her way of opposing me initially was to try to get me under her leadership. She wanted to license me as a minister of the gospel, and she wanted me to talk on the phone with her everyday, several times a day. She wanted to tell me how to think, who to marry, who I could be friends with, and she even went so far as to tell me that she'd only pray for me to have one child, because, according to her, *we had work to do*.

Please understand that opposition does not always come to you looking like opposition. Sometimes, the enemy uses friendly faces and what appears to be great opportunities to oppose your position in the Lord. Satan knows that God has given you a set of instructions, and he knows that God wants you to turn to Himself whenever new doors open so you won't go through the wrong ones. Satan also knows that it is the nature of the flesh to desire to be glorified, so Satan will use you against yourself. Satan's greatest weapon against you is you.

One of Satan's favorite moves against believers

is to position people around those believers
who will eventually oppose them. These
people come with friendly faces, helpful
intentions, and selfish motives. When a person
can only see how they can benefit off you, you
are not a human being to them. You are
nothing but another tool they're using to get
what they want out of life, and people like this
can be extremely dangerous. That's why it's
important to pray about everyone who comes
into your life, and to not allow anyone to
become someone you need in your life. Now
that I'm wiser and more alert, I've noticed that
most people who have evil motives come
looking for a place in my heart or my life that
they think I need help in. Some people will
show you their hearts' scars in hopes that you'll
show them yours. One such woman came
along after I'd been in business for a few years.
By this time, my business wasn't just a
business, it was a successful business; plus, I'd
grown in the things of the Lord, and I was
teaching people how to avoid the vultures that
like to go after Christian businesses. Even
though I didn't let her in my life, I got a

refreshing lesson on how wolves like to con their way into Christian ministries and businesses.

The woman sent me a message online asking me to call her. Now, this is a red flag in itself because I have websites, and any question she could possibly ask was likely covered on my website. Additionally, I had a contact form and my phone number on my sites, so her insistence that I call her told me a lot about her. She was a woman bearing a rebellious spirit, and she was trying to go around every other channel to get to me. She wanted to go around every wall she felt that would keep her and her motives away from me. I responded and told her that I don't call anyone, and that she would have to call me. I gave her my number, informing her that all of the information she could possibly want was on my website, nevertheless, she insisted on calling me.

When I answered the phone, I could hear that ever-so-familiar Jezebel spirit on her. I'd come across that spirit one too many times, to the point where I can now recognize it without even seeing it. She greeted me, and then, started trying to flatter me about my business. **Proverbs 29:5:** Those who flatter their neighbors are spreading nets for their feet.

I couldn't get a word in with her, so I held the line while she told me how great my business was, and how long she'd been following me. After the flattery session, she said to me that before she told me what she wanted, she wanted to share her story with me. I tried to interject, but she kept talking, so I tried to be polite and listen to her. She went on and on, telling me about her ministry, how it had gotten started, the opposition she'd faced along the way, and how her ministry's funds were now tied up. I knew what she wanted. She wanted me to see her as a success in the making, and she wanted me to do some work for her at no cost to her. I'd seen "her kind" plenty of times before, and I recognized her motives through her cunning words. As she testified, she kept stopping to compliment my business, my ministry, and my photos. I held the line, trying to be professional and polite because the time was ticking away, and her story seemed to always be at the beginning. Finally, after over an hour of talking, which I normally do not allow, she went on to ask me a ton of questions about how I'd gotten started. When I mentioned that I hadn't went to school for the things I was doing, she saw her opportunity. She started telling me that it was a good time to go back to school, especially since I am a woman. She said that she knew people who could help me out, but I politely declined her help, telling her that I have no reason to go to school. I have a successful business, I know how to build websites professionally, I'm a professional Graphic Designer, and everything I'd learned to do had come from God. Nevertheless, despite my rejection of her offer, she continued to insist that I go back to school so I could have a degree. She said the degree would open more doors for me, and again, I politely and respectfully disagreed. I've been hired by Web Designers to design sites they don't know how to design, I've been hired by Graphic Designers to create graphics they don't know how to create, and I was constantly learning more. On top of it all, I don't owe back any student loans because my Teacher was and still is the Holy Spirit. Every time I told her no, and explained that I'd be paying a school to teach me what I already knew, she would get even more offended. For her, it wasn't about me learning something new; it was about me getting a degree. What was supposed to be her asking a few questions about some services she wanted, turned into her aggressively trying to push me into something my spirit wasn't in agreement with. The more she realized that I wasn't budging, the more aggressive and angry she became. Her tone became condescending, and that spirit couldn't hide itself anymore. I finally got around to doing what I normally do with customers who try to get personal with me: I asked her what services did she need, apologizing for having to change the direction of our conversation, and telling her that I had other customers trying to call in. She didn't want anything. Angry, she got off the phone with me, and blocked me on social media.

145

What was her problem? She did something
that Jezebels commonly do with people who
underestimate the God in them. She started
trying to get me to base my worth and my
company's worth on a piece of paper, but when
she couldn't get me to budge, she became
offended. The problem was she didn't want to
pay me for any services. She wanted to find an
area of my life where she could insert herself,
hoping that I would become dependent on her.
To her, my unwillingness to listen to her advice
was a direct insult against her. There were too
many walls up that were guarding my
businesses and my ministry, and she couldn't
get around them. I knew my worth, therefore,
she couldn't redefine my worth, so she did
what most Jezebels do....she started trying to
speak word curses at me. She was opposition
manifested, and the mistake I'd made was
letting her talk for so long. Once I'd realized
that she wouldn't let me cut in, I should have
hung up the line, but I didn't. I ended up
being on the phone with that woman for an
hour and a half. I was so disappointed in
myself after that call because, again, I never let

people hold me on the line like that, especially since people who have a lot to say are often people with hidden agendas. Nevertheless, we got off the phone with her being angry because she'd put in more than an hour of her time trying to find a way to insert herself into my life, business, and ministry, only to have me reject her advances. I tell this story because it's a common scenario for many talented believers, especially the ones who don't know their worth. I've had too many talented babes in Christ to reach out to me, complaining about some man or woman who'd promised to help them, only to repeatedly use and condescend them. In most cases, they'd been intercepted by Jezebel spirits, and they were afraid to just cut those leaders off because they knew that separating from them meant they'd deal with verbal backlash from that person. They didn't know what rights they had or did not have, and many of them had been promised money and gifts that they were still waiting on. I had to be honest with them, and tell them they'd never see the money or gifts they'd been promised. The promises are nothing more than manipulative chains designed to keep them from walking away. The enemy knows what you *think* you need, and he'll offer you that in exchange for your will. You see, when you are dealing with controlling, manipulative people, they want you to operate in their will, only giving you the ability to make your own decisions when they deem fit. As a matter of fact, many controlling people will allow you to make your own decision about something, and this allowance is their reward to you for being obedient. Of course, we know that there is a demonic spirit in these people, but what many believers don't know is that a lot of leaders in the pulpits are controlled or used by demonic spirits. They see the people who are members of their ministries as their own personal tools, designed to get them to where they want to be in ministry. This goes for you as well. You need to pray before you affiliate yourself with a ministry, because if the leader of that ministry is controlling, manipulative, and selfishly ambitious, that leader will do everything in his or her power to destroy your reputation if you don't submit to that leader's control. The pastor I mentioned earlier who tried to license me under her ministry threatened to destroy my reputation, and not because I'd done something wrong or I'd done something to her. The problem was I'd stopped taking her calls and she'd realized that I was trying to distance myself from her. I'll never forget a conversation I had with her no less than a week before I started taking my distance from her. She'd called me, and midways through our conversation, she jokingly asked me in the most arrogant voice, "Am I controlling?" After her question, she started giggling, and I told her that she was. She was unrepentant, and that conversation let me know that not only was she was aware of her controlling ways, she took pride in being that way. After that conversation, I'd made up my mind to separate myself from her, but I didn't know how to do it without having some long, drawn out conversation with her, so I decided to just avoid her calls.

Opposition is something we all face, but it's how you look at it that will determine how you treat it. It's so easy to see the faces of the people the enemy is using to oppose you, but the truth is, your war is not with them. Your war is with whatever devil they have in them. **Ephesians 6:12 (NIV):** For our struggle is not against flesh and blood, but against the rulers, against the authorities, against the powers of this dark world, and against the spiritual forces of evil in the heavenly realms.

A form of opposition that many Christian Artists face are leaders who invite them to their churches, benefit financially off them, and then, don't give them anything to help with the expenses they'd accrued while traveling to those churches. This form of opposition was designed to discourage Artists from wanting to go any further in their ministries, but you've got to know that everyone doesn't think or behave like the leaders who've used and abused you. That's just a realm you have to go through to get to your next revelation and a deeper understanding about your gift. Some people get to that place, and turn back because they think that most leaders are hungry wolves who hide behind their priestly robes and glass pulpits. The first thing you have to do is get to the understanding you'll need to go beyond that realm of thinking, and get into a place where people can stop using you, and God can use you all the more. It goes without saying that you shouldn't see your ministry as an opportunity to make money, and I do understand that the lines between being used by man or used by God are often blurred. That's why you need to have an intimate relationship with God so you'll know which doors He's opened for you, as opposed to the doors the enemy is opening to hinder you. Neither you nor I can use our own understanding to discern every devil that confronts us, and we won't always choose the best doors to go through. Nevertheless, if we have an active relationship with God, we'll be able to hear Him and avoid those doors with golden doorknobs that promise to lead us to golden opportunities, doors that lead to humiliation, degradation, ridicule, persecution, false accusations, and the like.

Overcoming Opposition

One of the first keys to overcoming opposition
is to know who you are in the Lord, and to
know your own worth. You are purpose
manifested, meaning, you are not just a pretty
face and a beautiful voice. You are a spirit
being given an earthly body to perform a
certain task or series of tasks in the realm of the
earth. Every person you meet is either a
person who supports your position or a person
who opposes your position. Some people will
support your position silently, meaning, even
though they are not against you, they won't
stand up for you because they fear being
opposed themselves. Some people will oppose
your position silently, meaning, even though
they are not for you, they won't stand up
against you out of fear of being exposed
themselves. You've got to learn to discern who
is for you and who is against you. At the same
time, you've got to understand that not
everyone who says they're for you is for you.
Some of your greatest enemies will be the ones
standing on the sidelines, shouting your name
in support of you. That's because every devil
you meet has a certain rank, and it cannot

attack you until you are equivalent to or
greater than its rank. So, some people will
hang around you for years, but the minute you
step onto a platform that goes beyond their
understanding, whatever spirit is using them
will show itself, and it'll begin to oppose you
through them. And because you've been
friends with that person for years, you've likely
told that person things about yourself that
most folks don't know, and that's when your
"friend" will begin to use what you've told him
or her against you. I had to learn to stop
waiting on "friends" to show me their true
colors, and I started calling out their names in
prayer, asking the Lord to deliver me from
them if they were sent in my life by the enemy.
I also asked the Lord to re-position them in the
places He wanted them to be in my life if He
was the one who sent them. Understand that
some people who come into our lives and
oppose us were not sent by the devil. They
were sent by the Lord, but because we did not
consult with the Lord as to their roles and
responsibilities in our lives (and vice versa), we
gave them roles and positions that they were

not qualified to have. Anytime you do this, you will face opposition, since you've placed the right person in the wrong position, so the truth will oppose their positions.

And then, there's the obvious opposition, and this opposition comes from people who openly oppose our stances. They may mock us, ridicule us, and even attempt to confront us, but the key to bypassing these broken souls lies in your humility or lack thereof. If your heart is filled with pride, the enemy knows this, so he'll send people to openly and loudly oppose you because he knows you won't be able to resist defending yourself. He knows that with pride, you will seek to win the argument, not understanding that you are not fighting with flesh and blood; you are being opposed by a demonic spirit. With pride, you'll only see the person, and you'll oppose the person, and this empowers the spirit that is using that person because you've placed yourself on the same platform as that person.

Proverbs 24:6: Do not answer a fool according to his folly, or you yourself will be just like him.

One of the hats I wear is Web Design, and I remember when I'd first started off in Web Design. I'd built a website for my company, and I'd shared the link of the website on my Myspace page. A guy on my page wrote a condescending remark under the photo, and then, he proceeded to inbox me. He told me how it ticked him off that people like myself had never been to school for Web Design, but we thought we could just jump into that field. He said that unschooled Web Designers were unprofessional, and our work looked awful. He then went on to mention that he'd went to school for Web and Graphic Design, and people like myself were stealing his business. Even though I could understand his frustration, I couldn't agree with him because God had gifted me to do what I was doing, even though I was still in the infant stages of my career. I told him that God had given me the gift, and I humbly told him that I knew I wasn't the best, but I'd get there someday. *Of course, I'm paraphrasing and trying to remember*

the event as it happened. I then concluded my
email with "God bless you", and I left it at that.
I didn't insert pride, sarcasm, or any insults in
my response to him. I dealt with him humbly
and in love, and this broke that spirit of pride
off him. He responded by apologizing for his
behavior, stating that he'd tried to belittle me
with his words, and I'd responded by blessing
him. He thanked me for not coming after him
the way he'd come after me, and he offered to
teach me to professionally design sites
whenever I was ready. I was excited about the
opportunity, and glad that I'd responded in
love instead of responding out of offense.
Nevertheless, God would never allow me to
reach out to him because God wanted to teach
me everything I would come to know. He'd
already declared that no man or woman would
get the glory for anything I've done. All glory
belongs to God.

Did I handle that opposition well? Of course, I
did. I didn't give him the response he
deserved, but I gave him the response he
needed. He started off as opposition, but our

communication ended with him offering to help me better my position. Pride will always set you back, but a gentle response will always set you up for a blessing.

Proverbs 15:1: A gentle answer turns away wrath, but a harsh word stirs up anger.

Another form of opposition is the people we often enter romantic relationships with. The greatest weapon against a man's position is a wife who doesn't agree with it. The greatest weapon against a woman's position is a husband who's jealous of it. We can be gifted, talented, or anointed, and still be lost. Because we attract what we are, when we were broken, we found ourselves in the company of broken people who were fascinated by our talents. They were temporary acquaintances who found places in our hearts that they could insert themselves into, and they somehow became permanent fixtures in our lives, ministries, and careers. I can't tell you how many talented men and women of God I've come across who had a spouse at home opposing them every chance they got. Some

157

people will never reach their greatest potential, or even get a glimpse of it because of the spouses they have at home. Please know that when God has called you to the nations, the enemy is going to send folks after your anointing, and they will be attractive people who appear to support you. If you don't pray about them, and let God tell you who they are and if He's sent them, you'll end up married to a person whose assignment is to repeatedly bring you into places where the enemy can attack you.

Earlier on in this book, we discussed one form of opposition, and it usually comes from religious-minded people who support the world and its music, but will openly criticize Artists who promote and sell their music. These types of people are either not serving God or they haven't yet matured in the things of God, meaning, they don't know any better. If you allow their words to penetrate your heart, you will rethink your assignment, and it won't be long before you're walking away from every door God has opened for you and entering the doors they said you should go through. When I first started designing Bishop and Apostle Seals, I received some pretty wicked responses from women claiming to be women of God. One woman wrote me on Facebook, asking me why some leaders needed Bishop Seals, and I explained to her that they didn't need them, but it was something that had started with kings. She then went on to speak evil about my profession, even claiming that I'd go to hell if I didn't stop designing them. I looked at her photo, and I could see witchcraft all over her. She was wicked, and even though I wasn't completely mature in the things of God at that time, my eyes had been opened to see what and who I was dealing with. Another woman emailed me on Facebook, questioning my profession, and again, I told her it was something God gave me. She went on to criticize my work, and tried to speak a curse over me. Again, she was clearly a wicked woman, and like her predecessor, I blocked her. Not long after that, a woman who was on my friend's list on Facebook had posted a rebuke on my page.

She was obviously not too Facebook savvy, and she'd seen my Seal designs on her home page's wall. She assumed that I'd posted them to her personal page, so she posted to my wall, telling me not to post my designs on her page. Her post was full of flesh and anger, and then, she went from talking in first person to attempting to prophesy evil upon me. I knew that wasn't from God. She was a woman who didn't understand my profession, and she was a woman who likely didn't like to see other women succeed, so she came after me with fierce word curses that didn't have the power or the authority to penetrate my heart. I emailed her, rebuking her for her post to my wall, and letting her know that I hadn't posted anything to her wall. She needed to understand the difference between the home page's time-line versus the profile itself. After responding to her, I blocked her. These women were nothing but devil-possessed or devil-instructed women who had accepted the enemy's call on their lives to oppose the church, and anyone who did the will of God. How can I go so far as to say such a thing?

Overcoming Opposition

Every one of them attempted to speak curses at
me, instead of rebuking me in love. They
didn't have anything to rebuke (correct), so
they tapped into what they knew: to curse.
Blessings and curses cannot come from the
same heart, just as salt water and fresh water
cannot come from the same stream.
Matthew 7:18: A good tree cannot bear bad
fruit, and a bad tree cannot bear good fruit.

Always remind yourself that opposition is not
only normal, but it's necessary to get you past
your human emotions and into the place where
God can use you the most. Opposition exposes
the people around you who should not be in
your life. Opposition exposes what's on the
inside of you. How you handle conflict is a
reflection of what's in your heart. Opposition
imposes upon you to strive and pray to be a
better you. If the devil didn't oppose your
position, that could only mean your position
wasn't a threat to him. To overcome
opposition, you must overcome your flesh so
that you can be led by the Spirit of God and not
by your carnal being. To overcome

opposition, you've got to come to expect it, and at the same time, be prepared for it. How will you handle betrayal? Have you asked yourself this question, and considered the best routes to take to ensure God keeps the glory? How will you handle people who try to use and misuse your talents? Have you set some rules in place to ensure that you don't end up in the clutches of some selfishly ambitious leader who sees you as a paycheck? Have you thought of loving and creative ways to decline a person's offer to invite you to sing at their church? To oppose those who oppose you, you have to know your escape routes before the storm hits. If you are not prepared for the storm, you'll always tap into your flesh, and this will reflect poorly on your ministry.

General Tips for Advancement

In this chapter, I will share 20 random tips with you that will be beneficial to the growth, development, and expansion of your ministry. Please understand that some of this advice may be beneficial to you today, while some of it may be beneficial to you in the future. You need to understand what season you are in so that you don't plant the wrong seeds or pull up your blessings prematurely.

30 Tips to Advance Your Ministry

1. Open a Paypal account so that you can receive payments for your music. You will be signing up for many sites to sell your music on, and most of them will want to pay you through your own personal bank account or Paypal. You can use either or both, but you'll come to find that Paypal is really good with accepting payments, and Paypal offers buyer protection. Make sure that you

have some way to accept credit card payments because most of your online sales will come from people paying with credit or debit cards. If you ask them to send a check, you will lose the sale.

2. Be teachable and accept constructive criticism from whomever God places in your life. Be mindful of who's who so you can know the difference between constructive criticism as opposed to jealous criticism.

3. Make sure you have a Facebook fan page, and market it daily. If you don't have time to market the page, hire or barter with someone who can do it for you.

4. When getting your website designed, if at all possible, stay away from web templates, and get your own custom design. Your design should be as unique as you are. Some people recognize templates, and this may cheapen up your ministry in their views.

5. Join as many social media sites as possible.

6. When joining social media sites that allow for URL (domain) customization, try to use your ministry's name at all times. Be consistent. This helps with your Google listings.
7. Find sales agents. Give them a percentage of what is made on each sale.
8. Visit every small and large store in your city and surrounding areas and ask them if you can stock your music there. Offer them a percentage of the sales.
9. Join a charity or create one yourself. People love to support Artists who are giving back.
10. Interviews are good. Have a friend conduct an interview with you and post up the questions and responses online or set up one on the radio.
11. Ask your supporters to record themselves singing your music. Ask them to upload the videos to their YouTube pages, and to send them to you as well.
12. Ask your supporters to take photos of

themselves holding up a cardboard cutout or paper with your ministry's name and web link on it. Ask them to email those photos to you.

13. Be sure to get an EIN number. You're required by the IRS to report your earnings when you've earned $400 or more in a year.

14. Always take or purchase the pictures and videos from your show, and display whatever you're allowed to display on your website. This keeps the website fresh, and the viewers engaged.

15. It's expensive to have a Web Designer update your website every time you're invited to an event. My solution for my clients is to create a blog page for them to post about their own upcoming events. On their blog pages, they can upload flyers, answer questions, and keep their followers engaged.

16. Invest in your ministry and it will pay you back. Get the best equipment, and spare no expense when it comes to your ministry. Remember, how you treat

your gifting will determine how it treats you in return.

17. Ladies, always keep a neutral colored pair of flat, but stylish shoes in the trunk of your car, or in your tote bag. If the shoes you are wearing are too painful, or if the heel breaks, you'll have a backup with you at all times.

18. You can usually find great prices on domains from Godaddy. Now, you can go with other domain providers as well, but what I like about Godaddy is their prices are pretty much consistent year after year. Other domain providers that I've worked with have taken their prices up to as much as $35 when the time came for me to renew my domain. Right now (2015), domain names are about $12.99, but I rarely pay that amount for a .com domain name. Instead, I google "Godaddy coupon code" and I'm usually able to find a code for anywhere between 99 cents to $7.99.

19. Register with ASCAP. (American Society

of Composers, Authors, and Publishers) to license your music.

20. Increase your listings on Google by trading links with other websites. Be sure that you only trade links with websites that don't contradict or shed a bad light on the gospel (or your ministry) such as gambling, secular, or pornographic websites.

21. Stay busy. When dealing with major labels, one thing they ask is about your shows...past and present. If you aren't moving, they aren't going to move in your favor.

22. Create and send out a weekly newsletter. You should always appear to be busy, even when you're not.

23. Get an auto responder linked to your email. If you can't respond to the overflow of email, an auto responder will respond on your behalf.

24. Help out in your community. People love to support Artists who are making a difference.

25. Partner with a music distribution

company such as CD Baby, so you won't have to prepare, package, and ship every CD that's ordered. Of course, music distribution companies keep a percentage of the money earned on their site, but they also help to increase sales dramatically.

26. Buy books and read articles that will help you with your music ministry. There's a wealth of information to be had, but only a few Artists actually venture out to seek that information. One of the most dangerous mindsets an Artist can fall victim to is thinking he or she knows it all. A know-it-all is a person who's stopped growing up, and has started spreading out. What this means is they are not longer growing in wisdom, knowledge, or understanding, so they've become full of themselves. Because their egos have taken over their ministries, they start to become puffed up in their thinking, and they become argumentative anytime someone challenges what they believe or

introduces new information to them.

27. Be sure to copyright your music. Do not rely on the infamous "poor man's copyright" because it doesn't offer you as much protection as a registered copyright. A copyright, if filed online, is currently only $35. It's $65 if apply by mail. *This information is current for the year 2015. Prices may have changed over the months and years, and I am in no way responsible for price changes. Please check the U.S. Copyright website for current pricing and registration information.*

28. Make sure you get your bio, flyers, and web content proofread before you publish them. I've seen many Artists publish materials that were poorly written, and believe it or not, this affected their ministry.

29. Stay away from small-minded people. Let's face it. You are who you hang with, and in the music industry, your clique can be your pedestal or your downfall. The problem isn't with a class of people, so please don't mistake what

I'm saying. The problem is that small-minded people often single-handedly destroy their own careers. For example, I told you the story of an Artist I used to work with whose relative was destroying his career. His cousin spoke with much knowledge, and acted as if he was defending him, but in reality, it was clear to me and others that he was purposely sabotaging his career. He didn't want him to succeed because every time someone was interested in working with the aforementioned Artist, his cousin would speak to that person, and he would berate, threaten, and be belligerent with that person. He wanted to make it known that he was in charge and was to remain in charge, and that's because he was small-minded. Small-minded people have big plans for little people, meaning, they often can't see past themselves. Another example would be an Artist who doesn't have a great rapport with the local churches, event coordinators, and some of the

171

people in the music industry. That Artist is known to be dishonest, not show up to scheduled events, be late at scheduled events, or to be prideful. Artists who garner such a reputation have already poisoned their own ministries, and if you hang out with them, they will slowly poison your ministry. Surround yourself with people who inspire you, and people who are inspired by you.

30. Familiarity breeds contempt. One of the biggest mistakes I've seen many Artists and entrepreneurs make is hiring family and friends to start-up or run their ministries or businesses. Now, this is a good idea if God told you to hire them, but all too often, Artists hire familiar faces because they are comfortable with those people. That's a mistake. In music, you have to be taken outside your comfort zone again and again until you get comfortable at new heights. Family and friends will oftentimes encourage you to be who they think you

are, and not the Artist you could be, and of course, this is because they know you at a certain level. It's hard for people who know you to imagine you at great heights, so they will often see the potential in you to make their own names great and fatten up their own pockets. That's when they'll start trying to control your ministry because they're afraid that if you're left up to your own devices, you will destroy "their" opportunities to become as great as they believe they should be. This may sound harsh, but ask around. Many Artists have had their ministries torn down by familiar faces. It is better to work with people who don't know the "old you" or the person they think you are; that way, they can see your actual potential. The benefit of having a familiar face is they know what you like today, but what's going to happen tomorrow when you are no longer the same? You are scheduled to change, and that's why it's never a good idea to work with familiar faces *unless* God says otherwise.

Should You Start Your Own Label?

A lot of Artists ask the question: Should I start my own label? After waiting for years to get signed to a major or indie label, many Artists have ventured out to start their own labels, but is this a good idea? The answer to that question would depend on the following:

- Do you have enough money to *properly* start and run your own label?
- Do you have enough knowledge to start and *properly* run your own label?
- Do you have enough time to *properly* develop and manage your own label?
- Do you have access to the *professional* equipment you'll need to *professionally* develop the music and offset costs?
- Do you have the *professional* team you'll need to *properly* develop, start, run, maintain, and manage your own label?

175

Money

Let's face it. You need money to start, run, and maintain a label. Sure, it's easy to find a few people who'd be willing to join your team because they believe in your abilities, but in most cases, people who are not paid to do what they're doing usually quit or slack up within a year's time. That's because their bills keep coming every month, whether they're working or not. At the same time, you've got to understand the responsibilities of a label. Labels normally pay for their Artists' studio time, they pay the Artist royalties (in advance), they pay for almost everything associated with the production of their Artists' music. Studio time for one Artist alone could cost thousands of dollars. That's not to mention the Audio Engineer's fee to mix and master the music, the production costs, the packaging costs, and the distribution fees. Let's not forget the travel expenses accrued when your Artists are on tour. Then, there's the Artists' website, music video costs, photography, and the list goes on and on. This isn't to discourage you, it's to help you understand the responsibilities of a music label, so you don't go in with the wrong mindset.

A lot of people start their own labels because they want to say that they're signed to a label, or they want to say that they own their own label. I've met many people who were owners of their own labels, but in most cases, their labels didn't last long because they didn't have enough money to run those labels, or they were too cheap to invest in them. If you won't invest in yourself the way you should invest in yourself as an Artist, then, starting a label is not for you at this moment. In time, you may be ready, but starting and running a label requires faith, diligence, long-suffering, and money. Again, it's easy to find people around you who can supply you with the things you'll need, but they won't be willing to enter into any contractual agreements with you, seeing, as it is, that they're not being paid. And once another (paying) opportunity presents itself to them, they'll more than likely follow the money. So, if you want to start your own label, make sure you are financially able to do so. A lot of people start labels with no money, but their labels don't go anywhere, and they end up spending out more money than they're bringing in, and that's the opposite of being an Entrepreneur. Sure, in the beginning of a business, you will spend more money than you're bringing in, but most businesses look to turn a profit within the first year or two. This means you don't have five years to throw money into an empty well. You need to have a business plan in place, your connections in place, and the money you'll need to get it all done professionally. Don't just start a label; start a professional, profitable label, and this only works if you believe in your label enough to invest time and money in it.

Knowledge

I remember considering starting my own Christian label. After all, I'd worked with musicians before, and I knew a lot about the music industry. Nevertheless, I knew that I needed to learn more before investing into a "good idea". I utilized Google to see what I'd need to do to start and run a label, and I was overwhelmed by the amount of information that came up. How was I going to make time to learn everything that was before me? It was too much for me at that time, so I decided to back off and stay focused on what God had me doing.

You need knowledge to start and run a label. A lot of people think that starting a label is nothing more than picking out a catchy name, getting two or three people to agree to be under that label, launching a website for their new label, uploading a few tracks to their websites, and then, promoting their new site. They haven't the faintest clue as to what it means to start and run a label. As a matter of fact, had I started my label when I'd initially thought about launching one, I would've been one of those folks. Please understand that the music business is one of the shadiest businesses out there, and there are a lot of sharks in that pool looking to devour unknowledgeable Artists and the labels who sign them. These people are wordsmiths, and they are knowledgeable about the ins and outs

of the music business. They'll always look like
the answers to your prayers, but deep within
their hearts are selfish and wicked motives.
They steal the unlicensed music of the Artists
who are too cheap to license or copyright their
music, they present profitable opportunities for
the Artist, only so they'll profit off them, and
they steal every good idea that's thrown their
way, but not before shooting those ideas down.
The music industry is a profitable business,
and a man with knowledge of it can make a lot
of money from it. If you don't have the
knowledge you'll need to run a label, your
label will be nothing more than a vehicle
without an engine. Knowledge is the engine of
your label, so if you want to start a label, get as
much knowledge as you can, read as many
books as you can, and interview as many
knowledgeable (and reputable) people as you
can. The music industry is like a man who
owns a junk yard, and all of the uninformed
labels and Artists out there are the vehicles that
man uses to build his yard. He takes parts
(knowledge, music, lessons) from the labels
and people who don't know how to use those

parts, and he profits from them.

Time
Do you have the time to invest in starting and running a label? Investing an hour a day into your new or established label isn't enough. With a label, you need to be dedicated to the vision you have for that label, and this usually requires that you invest four or more hours a day building, developing, and promoting your label. You have to spend a lot of time making sure the Artists signed to your label have events to minister at. At the same time, you have to constantly speak with the Artists signed to your labels, making sure they are aware of the bookings they have and making sure they hold up their ends of whatever agreements they have. If an Artist is booked to show up at an event, and he's under a contractual agreement for that event, your label will be held legally, financially, and morally responsible if he does not show up. So, Artist managers have to spend a lot of time reaching out to and monitoring their Artists.

When I worked with secular Artists, I'd called myself managing an Artist, and there were many times that he was scheduled to perform, but he'd thrown a temper-tantrum outside the shows because they weren't honoring him the way he felt he should be honored. I would spend a lot of time on the phone with that Artist trying to talk him into just following their rules, and this cut into my own personal time.

If you've got a full time job and a family, you probably don't have the time you'll need to invest into a label, unless you have a knowledgeable team of people who can take some of that weight off you.

Equipment
Equipment pretty much ties in with costs, because, as I mentioned earlier, studio time is expensive. That's why a lot of people who venture out to start their own labels have their own in-house studios. Having your own studio cuts down on the costs big time because it enables your Artists to record their music in

your studio. At the same time, it presents you an opportunity to earn some extra money because a lot of people who have in-house studios rent out studio time to people who are not under their labels.

One of the guys I met who had his own label, not only had his own studio, but he had the equipment to mix and master the music himself. He was so resourceful that after hiring me to design his website, he started learning how to maintain his own site. Now, I wasn't happy about what he'd done to the site, but the point is...he was determined to offset costs by any means necessary.

Team
You need a team to properly run a label. Without a team, your label will be a one-man show, and you'll quickly find out just how difficult it is to manage. At the same time, promising to pay your team when the label starts turning a profit is not a good marketing plan. People have bills, and they won't stick around to wait for you to make good on your

promises. That's why you need to have something to offer your team; something they need in their day-to-day lives. Of course, most people will prefer money, but if you have something that's equal to or greater than what they feel they're putting into your label, many of them will work with you.

Having a professional and active team is the key to a label's success. There are a lot of talented people out there who want the opportunity to do something great, but simply acknowledging their talents isn't enough. You've got to honor their talents by paying them what they want to be paid, not what you think you should give them. I've had many opportunities to work with some indie labels, but I turned them down because I have my own ministry and my own business that takes up most of my time. I couldn't find the time to dedicate to building someone else's label, and waiting for a payday that would probably never come. Nevertheless, for me, it's not as much about the money as it is about the time. I have to dedicate my time to my own God-given assignment, and there are a lot of people who think as I think. They've got their hands full, and they can't abandon their own assignments to help another person fulfill theirs. The point is...make sure that the people you are working with are people who have the time, the talent, and the energy to work with you. At the same time, beware of people who don't have staying power. These are people who go from one business to another, learning what they can, and then leaving. They'll always take what they know and try to launch their own similar businesses. So, make sure your team is a team of God-sends, and not someone you went after just because they were knowledgeable. Pray about everyone; after all, your label is your business, and you have to mind it well.

It all boils down to how much of yourself you are willing to invest in a label. A lot of people start labels just to say they have labels, but having a label is pointless if it's not going anywhere. I have several businesses, and over the years, I've launched as many good ideas as

I have God ideas. The difference, I've found, is that with God ideas, I have everything I need on the inside of me to get the job done. With the good ideas, simply creating and launching the site was as far as I'd gotten. Once I caused the ideas to manifest as actual businesses, I didn't have anything else (time, money, or energy) to give to those businesses. I quickly lost interest in them, and I continued to focus on my God ideas. Make sure starting a label, for you, is a God idea, and if it's a good idea, ask the Lord if He will give you the permission and resources you'll need to merge that idea with your God-given assignment. In many cases, He will give you the desires of your heart, but please remember, He has a plan for you that's greater than your plan for yourself. If you want to cancel the delays that are keeping you from your promised land, try asking Him His will for you. If it's His will that you start a label, He will give you what you need to do so. If it's not His will, find out what He wants you to do; after all, that's where your success lies.

Steps to Starting Your Label

So, you've decided that starting a label is right for you. You've got what it takes to start up and run a Christian music label, and now, you simply want to know where to begin. First off, congratulations for wanting to create a label that focuses on the gospel. Most people chase secular labels because secular music has a larger audience, but our goal (as ministers of the gospel) is to change those numbers, and bring the souls back to Christ. People who choose secular music simply because they want more money and more views are people whose lost touch with what Christianity is all about. And that's not to be offensive to those of you who want to run a secular label; the point is we need more soldiers on the righteous side. We need people to use their gifts, talents, and anointings to show the world that the church is where they want to be, instead of teaching the church that the world is where they ought to be...*because it isn't.*

Starting and maintaining a label is a lot of hard work, and the process will discipline you if you don't become overwhelmed and quit, like so many people do. One of the keys to not quitting is investing enough money and time into what you're doing; that way, the value you place on your money and your time will be transferred to your label. People who invest more usually find it harder to quit because they've got a lot invested in their labels. People who don't invest a lot usually give up after a year or two; after all, they don't have that much invested into their labels, and they don't feel like maintaining those labels is worth anymore of their time. In other words, they have one of the characteristics often associated with poverty and that is: giving a little and expecting a lot in return.

Below, are 20 tips to starting your own label:
1. Choose the name of your new label. Make sure the name is catchy and it isn't already in use.
2. Go ahead and purchase your domain name for your website. This locks the name in for you and helps you to start preparing for the journey.

3. Create a business plan. Businesses that have business plans are 75% more likely to succeed than the ones that don't.

4. Decide what type of sound and Artists you want under your label, and create a plan that helps you to stand out from other labels. You never want to blend in with the many independent labels out there. The key to success is standing out.

5. Do a projection of your costs, and start saving money. In today's market, it's pretty easy to forecast how much you'll need to spend because we have the Internet. As long as you know what you need, you can find price projections.

6. Estimate how much money you intend to bring in. Please know that the first few years are often unprofitable, and you may find that you're spending out more than you're bringing in. But the best thing to do is estimate how long it'll take you to get everything and everyone you'll need, and then, you can count everything after the projected date as a

time you should be seeing a profit. Once you know how much you should be bringing in, you'll be better at managing your costs.

7. Get your legals taken care of. Register with the I.R.S. so that you can get your EIN number, and your business will be recorded in their system. Also check with your state tax office to see if there's anything else you need to do to register your business in your state.

8. Look for legal representation. You need a lawyer because you're likely going to be dealing with contractual agreements, dishonest people, and sometimes, not so honorary Artists. People don't respond well to verbal threats, but they will usually respond to lawyers.

9. Get your contractual agreements in place. You need template agreements that you'll use with all of your Artists, and you need customizable agreements that you'll use with your team. The reason you need custom agreements for team members is some people will have

their own terms, and you may be willing to allow those terms if they don't put you at risk, cost you extra money, or if you feel they're worth what they're asking for.

10. Develop your team. The team is just as important as the business itself. Without a team, your label will be nothing more than a vehicle without an engine.

11. Find or set up a recording studio. Your Artists need somewhere to record their music, so you need to have a studio picked out or set up before you start looking for Artists.

12. Get your logo created. Your logo is your online and offline representative, and it helps you to establish your own unique look.

13. Visit some local music stores and ask them what you'll need to sell your label's music in their stores. You need this information in advance, rather than waiting until you have an album in the making or an album that's already

finished.

14. Find online (and offline) distribution channels. Companies like Amazon, CD Baby, and other online sources are great places to sell your music. Go ahead and set up your account with as many online distribution channels as possible, and review their policies so you'll know what they need from you.

15. Build your website. Let's face it. You can't get the Artists to take you seriously if you don't have a website. Artists want to be a part of something real, and not just something you're dreaming up. They need to know that you've got the legals together, and the business is already established, otherwise, they'll smile and nod their head at the idea, but they won't give you or your label a second thought.

16. Identify your target audiences, or each Artists' target audience.

17. Send out press releases, and reach out to some local and online media reporting sources. Your label needs exposure if

you want it to succeed.

18. Get your business cards ready so you can hand them out whenever you meet new people.

19. Go to some events so you can listen to and get to know the local Artists in your area. This will also help you to determine the sound you want and what sound or image you don't want.

20. Start off by focusing on one Artists' album at a time. That way, you don't get overwhelmed. Additionally, you'll be able to start getting a feel of the process you'll go through to record, package, and distribute the music.

Bonus: If you really want to look professional and get more attention, be sure to set up a toll free number for your label. When people see toll free numbers, they automatically link success to those numbers, so they'll be more inclined to work with someone who has a toll free number than someone who has a local number. A lot of labels forgo getting toll free numbers because they don't want to pay for them, but you have to spend money if you intend to make money. People who go into business thinking they'll spend a little and earn a lot in return are oftentimes delusional, but people who go in with success on their minds are people who have come to realize that success has a cost. The ones who are willing to pay the price for success are the ones who will usually get it. In business, I've come across a lot of Entrepreneurs who have been in business for years, and they aren't even making one thousand dollars annually. What do they all have in common? They refuse to invest.

An 800 number can cost you around $200 a year and up. What I did for my business was buy a toll free number, and pay it out for the year; that way, I don't have to deal with the monthly costs. A great place to get a toll free number is ringcentral.com.

Helpful Links to Propel Your Ministry

Social Media

Of course, you should be on every popular social media site there is, unless it's a profane or pagan site. Below, you'll find a list of some of today's (2015) most popular sites. Please note that this is not a complete list because I've only listed the sites that have been around for a while, or sites I think will be around for a while. A lot of sites for musicians close after a couple of years, so it's wise for you to search for more links in addition to the links below. Of course, you may have to add the www prefix.

Popular Social Media Sites
Facebook
Link: facebook.com
Why Facebook?: Currently, Facebook is the largest and most popular social media site on

the live Internet, boasting of more than 1.3 billion users as of 2015.

Facebook is a great place to share your music, collaborate with other Artists, and build your listener base.

Twitter

Link: twitter.com

Why Twitter?: Twitter is also a great place to share your music, keep your listeners updated with upcoming shows, and much more. Twitter is also another one of today's largest social media sites. Currently, Twitter boasts of more than 600 million users.

Instagram

Link: instagram.com

Why Instagram?: Instagram has grown and continues to grow in popularity. Instagram allows you to share photos and videos to your followers. It's a great place to show your listeners that you are busy. Currently, Instagram boasts of more than 300 million users.

Pinterest

Link: pinterest.com

Why Pinterest?: On Pinterest, you can also upload images or videos of your current or past shows. Currently, Pinterest has more than 70 million users.

LinkedIn

Link: linkedin.com

Why LinkedIn?: LinkedIn is business-oriented and focused on helping you to strengthen your relationships with your current followers. It's also a great place to post your resume, look for talent, and promote the business end of your ministry.

Google Plus+

Link: plus.google.com

Why Google Plus+?: Google has been around for a while, and it will continue to flourish in the coming years because Google wants a share of every major pie that's being served. Google Plus+ is a great place to find or add new followers, as well as promote your music. Google Plus+ is also reported to have just as many followers as Twitter.

Tumblr
Link: tumblr.com
Why Tumblr?: Tumblr is a microblogging platform that boasts of more than 227 million blog users. Blogging is a great way to connect to your listeners, promote your music, and keep your listeners updated with your ministry's schedule.

VK
Link: vk.com
Why VK?: Vk.com is being hailed as the largest European social network, boasting of more than 100 million users. If you want to share your music around the world, VK is a great place to start. VK is very similar to Facebook.

Vine
Link: vine.com
Why Vine?: Vine is an innovative network that allows its users to upload videos that are up to six seconds in length. This is a great place to interact with your listeners through the use of

videos, and Vine is a great place to display your video bloopers. With more than 13 million users, Vine is quickly ascending the social media charts day after day.

Other Helpful Links
U.S. Copyright
Link: copyright.gov
Why the U.S. Copyright office?: Your music needs to be copyrighted, and this is where you'll have to go to get it done. Please note that currently (2015), it's $35 to file a copyright online, but it's $65 to file by mail. It is also better to file online because the application is approved faster. Another great thing is you can copyright more than one song at a time for only $55, and this will save you a ton of money. How important is a copyright? When I worked with secular Artists, I'd gotten a call early one morning from an Artist I was working with, and he was livid. "Turn on your television!" he exclaimed. He had me to go to one of today's most popular channels, and when I turned to the channel, an Artist was performing a song to an all-too-familiar beat.

"That's my beat, and he's using some of my lyrics!" yelled the Artist. Unfortunately, this is a familiar scenario with so many largely unknown Artists. Their music is stolen, and oftentimes, by the major players in the music industry. Why is this? Because a lot of Artists don't copyright their music, even though, they are somewhat protected by what is referred to as a "poor man's copyright". Secondly, most little known Artists are poor, and they don't have any knowledge as to what they ought to do to claim their music. They are often intimated by the big names who perform their songs, so, all too often, they'll simply pout and complain as another Artist performs and earns from their hard work. You need a registered Copyright because it offers more protection than a "poor man's copyright", and at the same time, should someone steal your music and earn from it, in addition to suing them for Copyright infringement, you can sue them to get back the money they've made off your song.

Broadcast Music Inc. (BMI)

Link: bmi.com

Why Broadcast Music, Incorporated?:
According to BMI's website, *BMI is the bridge*
between songwriters and the businesses and
organizations that want to play their music
publicly. As a global leader in music rights
management, BMI serves as an advocate for the
value of music, representing more than 8.5 million
musical works created and owned by more than
650,000 songwriters, composers and music
publishers. (Ref: BMI.com)

The American Society of Composers, Authors, and Publishers (ASCAP)

Link: ascap.com

Why ASCAP?: According to their website,
ASCAP is: *the American Society of Composers,*
Authors and Publishers (ASCAP), a membership
association of more than 525,000 US composers,
songwriters, lyricists and music publishers of every
kind of music. Through agreements with affiliated
international societies, we also represent hundreds
of thousands of music creators worldwide. We are
the only US performing rights organization created
and controlled by composers, songwriters and

music publishers, with a Board of Directors elected by and from our membership.

We protect the rights of ASCAP members by licensing and distributing royalties for the non-dramatic public performances of their copyrighted works. Our licensees encompass all who want to perform copyrighted music publicly. We make giving and obtaining permission to perform music simple for both creators and music users. (Ref: ASCAP.com)

Society of European Stage Authors and Composers (SESAC)

Link: sesac.com

Why SESAC? The following description of SESAC and their services were taken from their website: *SESAC utilizes a selective process when affiliating songwriters and publishers, resulting in a level of service and attention unparalleled in the industry. With an international reach and a vast repertory that spans virtually every genre of music, SESAC is the most innovative and technologically adept of the nation's performing rights organizations.*

SESAC currently licenses the public performances of more than 400,000 songs on behalf of its 30,000 affiliated songwriters, composers, and music publishers. (Ref: SESAC.com)

CDBaby
Link: cdbaby.com
Why CDBaby?: CDBaby is a great music distribution channel for indie Artists to sell their music. CDBaby even packages physical copies and sends them to the buyers for you. Let CDBaby, or whatever music distribution company of your choice, do all the hard work for you.

Livestream
Link: livestream.com
Why Livestream?: Livestream lets you post your events live over the Internet. This is especially good for people who can't make it to your shows because they are in other states, other countries, or they may be physically incapacitated.

Hootsuite

Link: hootsuite.com

Why Hootsuite?: Hootsuite allows you to post to several of your social network pages at one time. You can schedule posts and pretty much interact with people using one gadget. This is especially good for Artists who have profiles on several social media platforms, and want to keep the page content fresh and their listeners engaged. There are other companies like Hootsuite, so definitely check around to find which is better for you.

MailChimp

Link: mailchimp.com

Why MailChimp?: MailChimp stores the email addresses of your followers, and allows you to send customizable, attractive newsletters to your subscribers. Keep your listeners abreast of what's going on in your ministry, your event schedule, or send encouragement using MailChimp.

TopSpin

Link: topspinmedia.com

Why TopSpin?: *According to their Website,*

Topspin is: The direct-to-fan sales and marketing platform chosen by creative professionals who want to promote and sell films, albums, merch, tickets, & more. Topspin Media is the leading provider of sales and marketing software for musicians, filmmakers, and other creative professionals. (Ref: topspinmedia.com).

Blogger

Link: blogger.com

Why Blogger?: I personally recommend Blogger because first, it's free. Secondly, you can build an attractive blog, connect your domain name to that blog, and promote your blog using your Google profile. Blogger is currently owned by Google, so whenever people follow you on Google, they will automatically be linked to your profile. *Did I mention that it's free?* If you're not a great designer, let someone else put together a design for you, and blog away.

Wordpress

Link: wordpress.com

Why Wordpress?: Wordpress is a great

alternative to Blogger because it offers you the ability to use plugins to create cost effective, brilliantly designed, and fully functional sites. Unlike Blogger, however, Wordpress (without the advertisements) isn't free. If you use their free version, you cannot connect your domain to your site. You can create better looking sites with Wordpress than you can with Blogger, and unlike Blogger, Wordpress is largely used by Web Designers to create some really great-looking sites. Blogger is mainly used for blogs. If you don't mind shelling out the cash, Wordpress is a more attractive and functional option than Blogger.

Amazon
Link: amazon.com
Why Amazon?: Amazon is a great place to sell your music, plus, in 2014, it was reported that Amazon had over 240 million users, making it one of the most profitable online stores on the Internet.

ClickBank
Link: clickbank.com

Why ClickBank?: ClickBank allows you to sell digital content, it processes the payments itself, and helps you keep track of your sales. Not to mention, Clickbank has sellers who will sell your music for you for a small, agreed upon fee.

Other Helpful Links to Use for Music Promotion

Twit Music: twitmusic.com

Mp3: mp3.com

Spotify: spotify.com

SoundCloud: soundcloud.com

Reverb Nation: reverbnation.com

OurStage: ourstage.com

OurWave: ourwave.com

FanBridge: fanbridge.com

Kompoz: kompoz.com

BandCamp: bandcamp.com

YouTube: youtube.com

GodTube: godtube.com

iTunes: itunes.com

Vimeo: vimeo.com

TubeMogul: tubemogul.com

Lastfm: last.fm

Helpful Links to Propel Your Ministry

Blipfm: blip.fm
TheSixtyOne: thesixtyone.com
Pandora: pandora.com
Spotify: spotify.com

www.ingramcontent.com/pod-product-compliance
Lightning Source LLC
Chambersburg PA
CBHW060236050426
42448CB00009B/1468